Dr Jennifer Swanston and Dr Katherine Hodson

We are clinical psychologists who specialise in working with young people and their families. We are also both parents ourselves and have personal experience of the highs and lows of parenting.

We worked in the same UK National Health Service at various times, supporting young people and families who did not engage with typical behavioural approaches. This meant that we had to adapt our style to make sure we fully met the young people's needs, recognising that many had very difficult, sometimes traumatic experiences or had a particular way of seeing the world. This is how we originally connected, realising that we shared many similarities in our practice, such as flexibility, patience, the willingness to learn from our families and, above all, compassion. Over time, we both moved into private practice. This gave us the freedom to explore different therapeutic approaches, based upon the needs of each family and young person. Compassion-focused therapy was the glue that linked everything together for us.

We noticed a lack of books on compassionate parenting, despite parents' growing need for support. Therefore, our goal with this book was to share this compassionate parenting approach in as reader-friendly a way as possible.

We also roped in Katherine's teenage son, who provided us with some illustrations to help capture the essence of what we are saying and bring a little fun into the crazy world of parenting.

THE COMPASSIONATE MIND APPROACH

The self-help books in this series are based on compassion focused therapy (CFT, developed by series editor Paul Gilbert). This brings together an understanding of how our mind can cause us difficulties but also provides us with a powerful solution in the shape of mindfulness and compassion. It teaches ways to stimulate the part of the brain connected with kindness, warmth, compassion and safeness, and to calm the part that makes us feel anxious, angry, sad or depressed.

THE COMPASSIONATE PARENTING WORKBOOK

Using compassion to help tailor parenting to every unique child

DR JENNIFER SWANSTON
AND KATHERINE HODSON

ROBINSON

ROBINSON

First published in Great Britain in 2025 by Robinson

Copyright © Jennifer Swanston and Katherine Hodson, 2025

Illustrations by Will Hodson

Diagrams on pp. 8, 13, 39, 40, 47, 63, 73, 81, 86, 97, 99, 118, 149
and 219 by Liane Payne

1 3 5 7 9 10 8 6 4 2

A CIP catalogue record for this book is available from the British Library.

ISBN: 978-1-47214-974-9

Typeset in Palatino by Initial Typesetting Services, Edinburgh
Printed and bound in Great Britain by Bell & Bain Ltd, Glasgow

Papers used by Robinson are from well-managed forests and other responsible sources.

Robinson
An imprint of
Little, Brown Book Group
Carmelite House
50 Victoria Embankment
London EC4Y 0DZ

The authorised representative
in the EEA is
Hachette Ireland
8 Castlecourt Centre
Dublin 15, D15 XTP3, Ireland
(email: info@hbgi.ie)

An Hachette UK Company
www.hachette.co.uk

www.littlebrown.co.uk

Contents

Foreword by Professor Paul Gilbert

It is interesting becoming a grandparent and looking back on how I parented my own children. My grandmother, who was a parent from the 1920s to 40s, would say, 'Parenting is fairly straightforward. Children just need to feel safe and loved.' There is indeed wisdom to that, but making this a reality can be harder than we realise. There were certainly many causes of stress in earlier times but, gosh, how things have changed in the last eighty years – not least because there are now lots of studies about the impact parenting has on our children's psychological and physical development. In addition, we are now in a world of mobile phones, internet, social media and multiple television channels.

The problem is, we are trying to parent our children in totally abnormal environments. For millions of years, we lived in small groups of hunter-gatherers in which children were brought up by the community. A distressed child, or one looking for play, was just as likely to go to an aunt or uncle who lived only yards away as to their parent. We no longer live in open, collective spaces, where we can move in and out of our dwellings freely. Instead, we live in constructed boxes called houses and flats where it can be impossible to get away from each other, and friends and relatives are a lot more than just a few steps away. To put this another way, the stresses of child-rearing are not distributed through networks but placed much more directly on one or a couple of individuals. This type of stress can easily give rise to a sense of entrapment and simply wanting to get away, as well as to feelings of loneliness and isolation.

Drs Swanston and Hodson help us see these key themes about how and why parenting in the modern world, in spite of all the medical advances, can be difficult, tricky, stressful and distressing. Although the folksy guidance of grandmothers is useful and kindly meant, it can also set us up to have unrealistic expectations not equipped for the pressures and challenges of modern living. Not only are there stresses linked to poverty but also to managing complex roles and demands. We are called on to guide and help our children cope with the increasing competitive pressures of school, keeping up with constant new technologies and fashions, and with various invasive forms of social media that undermine rather than promote confidence. Modelling compassion means we can help our children not be over-absorbed in the storms of early life.

Although interest in compassionate ways of living are ancient, the last thirty years have seen an extraordinary development in our understanding of how compassion can affect our brains and bodies, our sense of self and relationships. Crucially, *The Compassionate Parenting Workbook* draws heavily on the science of compassion and offers important insights into how and why it can be very difficult even to want to be compassionate.

The authors make clear that compassion is about the way we are sensitive to life's problems, distress, needs, disappointments and setbacks, with an approach that doesn't undermine our experiences or lead to avoidance, but enables us to face these challenges and work out what best to do. Often compassion requires courage because we are moving towards things that are painful or difficult. It also requires wisdom because we have to work out how to address difficulties in a way that is going to be helpful rather than well-intended but ultimately unhelpful.

Crucial to parenting, and laid out clearly in this book, is recognising that none of us chose to be here with a particular gender, ethnicity and set of talents (or lack of them). We did not choose anything about our brain nor the emotions and dispositions that emerge from it. How many of us would like to be calmer when actually our brain insists on going into a spin of anxiety or frustration? How many of us would like to stay perfectly in control when our children are having a tantrum at the point we have to take them to school? In fact, if you think about it, none of the emotions that cause us distress are ones we actually choose. Compassion helps us understand that we experience what we experience because of how DNA has built our tricky brains. So that's not our fault. The key question is, can we teach ourselves how our brain generates these emotions and motives? What's the best way of working with a brain that can create havoc in our minds against our will?

This is where compassion comes in, because it helps us to back away from blaming and shaming and to bring to the fore genuine care and concern about our minds. Rather than being rushed along by the stresses of life, our disappointments in ourselves or self-criticisms, a compassionate mind can guide us through these.

Drs Swanston and Hodson write clearly about things that, as a parent, I wish I had known over forty years ago. They have written a lovely guide for parents on how to be compassionate, and to see that compassion is not the same as kindness or niceness (though these are good things too). By making compassion central to our parenting, they show us how to strengthen our relationship with our child (who has also been built by DNA and has a tricky brain that can be immature, needy and impulsive). Compassionate parenting is also a way of helping our children understand the nature of compassion as they move through childhood into adolescence. Making it central to their self, identity and way of living is so important for their wellbeing and relationships.

The essence of compassionate parenting is understanding why we have troubling emotions; that sometimes we just want to get away and not have to be a parent anymore; that sometimes we become more frustrated than we feel comfortable with; and that sometimes we may feel disappointment because our children are not the way we want them to be or thought they would be. Compassion helps us enable our children to unfold as themselves even when this is not always so easy, helping us to ride these realities and learn from them.

Professor Paul Gilbert PhD FBPsS OBE

January 2025

1 Compassionate Parenting

An Introduction

Most of us hear opinions about parenting before we become parents ourselves – many of which are focused on the idea that parenting is 'the best job in the world'. While there is no doubt that being a parent brings wonderful experiences and memories, and can be truly special . . .

Parenting can also be tough and it can trigger some of our difficult emotions.

And it doesn't matter what people (including our own parents!) say to warn us before we become a parent, parenting is harder than we expect and possibly the hardest job in the world.

Many people have commented on this over the years, often using humour to highlight their message. Some of our favourites are:

'The thing about parenting rules is there aren't any.
That's what makes it so difficult.'

Ewan McGregor (Scottish actor)

'Having children is like living in a frat house – nobody sleeps,
everything's broken, and there's a lot of throwing up.'

Ray Romano (American actor and comedian)

*'My biggest parenting conundrum: why is it so hard to put
someone who is already sleepy to sleep?'*

Chrissy Teigen (American model)

A BPI Network Survey in 2018 found that out of two thousand parents in the US and Canada, 88% reported believing that parenting today is harder than when they were growing up. Worryingly, 63% of the parents surveyed were experiencing parental burnout and 40% of these rated this burnout as having a significantly negative impact upon their lives. This tells us that it is common to find parenting difficult, which may relate to the following reasons:

- Humans are naturally group-living animals and in our past (e.g. when we lived in small hunter–gatherer groups), we would have parented in a community, not in isolation. You may have heard the saying, 'It takes a village to raise a child.' But this no longer happens for most people in our modern world

- Parents now tend to have less contact with babies and young children before having children themselves, which can make it difficult to know how to deal with the inevitable struggles of parenting

- Parents are bombarded with information on social media and from scientific research. This may set unrealistic expectations (e.g. losing baby weight within three weeks of giving birth) and give conflicting data on what you should and shouldn't be doing as you parent. For example, we are told not to feed our children solids before six months, but we are also told to feed our children peanuts from four months to reduce the risk of a nut allergy

From our combined years of experience supporting children, parents and families, we are acutely aware that there is no one model that fits all young people when it comes to parenting strategies and techniques. What can be incredibly helpful for one child simply does not work well with another.

Why do I need to use compassionate parenting?

It is natural to ask the question, 'Why should I read *this* book?', given the great number of parenting books available to buy, plus the parenting blogs and online resources that can be accessed relatively easily. We believe that the compassionate parenting approach differs from other parenting books and materials you have read in the past. Compassion is a motivational system that organises how the brain thinks and how the body responds, building on our basic desire to be caring. It gives us an approach to turn to when things get tricky. This helps you tailor your parenting approach to best suit your needs and those of your child.

The more traditional parenting strategies proposed over the years primarily focus on changing parental responses to children's behaviour. One example of this is using reward systems (such as sticker charts) to reward our children when they act in a helpful or positive way, to encourage our children to undertake more of this behaviour. These interventions have been researched and there is good evidence to show that they are helpful in reducing children's social, emotional and behavioural problems. However, recent research has shown that adding compassion to these parenting approaches can have even more of an impact. For example, a study in Vietnam looked at supporting grandparents who were greatly involved in bringing up their grandchildren. This study showed that adding a compassion-focused module to the more traditional parenting programme resulted in a significant reduction in the conflicts and tensions that arose between these grandparents and the children's parents. The same positive effect was also observed in the children's behaviour.

What is compassion?

Our model for parenting is based on the compassion-focused therapy approach proposed by Professor Paul Gilbert over twenty years ago, who has been developing it ever since. A great deal of research has been done into this approach and it is based on *evidence* and our knowledge of evolution, the body, brain (neuroscience), social development and behaviour (psychology).

Compassion-focused therapy integrates various ideas and approaches with compassion. But what is compassion?

Compassion comprises several elements:

- We notice and pick up on the cues of suffering or need that may be happening to ourselves or to others, including our children

- We recognise that suffering is universal – everyone faces tough times throughout their lives

- We feel sympathy and often concern for the person who is finding something difficult

- We may have to tolerate our own distress when spotting the distress in another person or in ourselves
- We are motivated to work out what to do that will be helpful to ease the suffering

So, overall, we can define compassion as:

A caring motivation that makes us sensitive to the suffering in ourselves and others, with a commitment to trying to relieve and prevent the suffering.

Compassion has three core components, which we will describe in more detail in this book:

1. Wisdom – being in tune with our children's needs and working out the parenting actions that are likely to be most helpful
2. Strength to face difficult emotions and parenting situations, rather than avoiding them
3. The caring commitment – to reduce distress in a way that is helpful and not harmful to us and our children. We may use passive caring actions (such as cuddling and comforting our children) or active forms of caring (such as giving our children specific strategies to help them in a difficult moment)

A common misconception is that compassion is merely being kind. Compassion can involve kindness, but at other times it may be more about being courageous and strong.

Take these examples:

- A nurse supporting a patient with a highly infectious disease, such as Ebola
- Firefighters running into a burning building during 9/11 in New York

How would you describe the actions of the nurse and firefighters?

Compassion is not weak, indulgent or selfish. It is wise, strong and courageous.

Being compassionate is hard work and involves many skills, including how to pay attention to distress, being motivated to respond to a person's distress, and having sympathy and empathy.

In this book, we will at times ask you to consider your own experiences, emotions and responses, and this can be hard to do. We will be guiding you towards understanding situations in a way that is not harsh or critical but, rather, is compassionate to yourself and to your children.

Don't be fooled. There are times when being critical and harsh can be dressed up as compassion. We cannot change our brains. We cannot change our emotions. We *all* feel anxious, angry, shameful, guilty and sad at times. We can be our own worst critic. This is part of being human.

There is an old legend called The Story of the Two Wolves. One day a grandfather was playing with his young grandson while telling him about the internal struggles we all have. He tells his grandson that there are two wolves that fight inside each of us. One wolf is kind, compassionate, joyful, wise, faithful, hopeful and caring. The other wolf is vengeful, angry, resentful, self-pitying and scared. Listening carefully, the grandson, asks his grandfather, 'Which wolf wins, Grandfather?' The grandfather smiled and said, 'The one you feed.'

What we are proposing is that we take a *compassionate* approach to all of this. Understanding our emotions, behaviour and experiences *compassionately*, thinking about what would be helpful and unhelpful in a situation, and using our wisdom and strength to put compassionate parenting strategies in place for ourselves and for our children.

Compassion moves in three directions:

- Compassion towards others – e.g. treating other people, including our children, in a compassionate way

- Being able to receive compassion from others – e.g. taking on board praise and the kind or wise words of others

- Compassion for oneself – e.g. being able to treat yourself compassionately

But what is compassionate parenting?

We live in a world that is rife with criticism – of ourselves, from others and to others. One look at social media or parliamentary question time shows us this. Unfortunately, this critical environment has a huge impact upon our wellbeing, with self-criticism leading to anxiety, guilt, sadness, shame and hopelessness. This naturally makes parenting feel harder.

However, when we are compassionate with ourselves, we are often more emotionally resilient and have lower stress levels and healthier relationships. Self-compassion is strongly linked to mental health. Being more compassionate gives us a greater sense of perceived personal control of our lives. This is important, as studies show that compassion has a positive impact on our awareness of our own distress, even when our children are struggling (e.g. anxiety, social withdrawal, tummy aches and headaches).

Research shows us that repeated experiences of name calling, smacking or other critical or shaming parenting techniques can result in children becoming fearful of compassion – for themselves, for others and from others. The same researchers also discovered that children experiencing warmth and a sense of safety from their parents or caregivers had a reduced risk of being fearful of compassion later on in their lives. And this is important to keep in mind, because fearing compassion can increase the chance of developing various mental health and wellbeing difficulties in adulthood, including anxiety, depression, obsessive compulsive disorder and loneliness. Therefore, in every strategy we suggest, compassion needs to underpin it.

So, we are here to introduce compassion to your life – to yourself, to you as a parent and in your approach to your child. Hopefully, in the future, this will mean your child will adopt this way of relating to themselves and to others, too.

We will now focus on the science and evidence behind this compassionate parenting approach. We have tried to give you the highlights, but if you want to learn more, then various links and further resources are provided at the end of the book.

Evolution and the brain

Our brains are complex. We know that evolution has shaped us and our brains. A single cell organism evolved over millions and millions of years into the common ancestors we share with a fish, frog, crocodile, rat, rhesus monkey and chimpanzee before evolving into our human body and brain.

Essentially, there are aspects of our brain we might call an 'old' brain, which have evolved over many millions of years. Plus, us humans also have a relatively 'new' brain. The old brain deals with survival – seeking food, avoiding harm, reproducing, thinking about our status, our emotions (anger, anxiety, sadness, joy) and our behaviours (e.g. urges to fight, flight or freeze, or to care). Our new brain is able to imagine, plan, ruminate, think about others and monitor ourselves. This rather unhelpful mix of old and new brain enables us to think about and imagine worst-case scenarios and also to criticise ourselves in the process, which can cause us additional distress as parents.

Imagine the following examples:

Example 1

You come home from work and smell burning. You call the fire brigade and they find that your grill had been left on, causing tiny pieces of fat on the stove to smoke. After the stove is turned off and with good ventilation, the burning smell starts to fade. Your house is OK. You find out that your husband accidentally knocked the grill when he was cleaning it earlier in the day, causing it to turn on. What would be running through your mind now? How would you feel?

Example 2

You are at a park with your two children. You take your eyes off one of them to focus on putting the younger one in the swing. When you look back, your older child has disappeared. You run around frantically searching – it feels like hours have gone by. Luckily, after five minutes, someone finds your child. They had wandered off and got a bit lost.

In these examples, two unpleasant, accidental situations luckily turned out OK. But in these sorts of scenarios, our brain tends to engage in what we call old brain/new brain loops. This leaves us feeling anxious and angry, even when you/others/property are safe. For example, there may have been new brain imaginative thoughts running through our minds, such as: 'What if we had been an hour later?', 'Why weren't there any adults around?', 'What if this happens again?' or 'What if that person had not found my child or my child had been taken?' You may have felt many things, like anger, shame, guilt and anxiety.

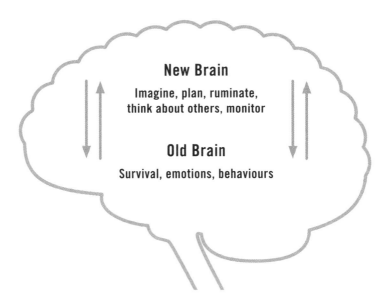

New Brain
Imagine, plan, ruminate,
think about others, monitor

Old Brain
Survival, emotions, behaviours

If we think about a zebra being chased by a lion, the lucky zebra would return to a calm state once it had outrun the lion. Unlike us humans, it would not engage in the same process of rumination or worry after the chase had ended. This is because a zebra only has an old brain and not a new one. Due to our new brains, we continue to stay in a high state of anxiety.

We will probably ruminate about what might have happened and then start to worry about the future (Will it happen again? How could I have let this happen?). As parents, these old brain/new brain loops can cause us to beat ourselves up, doubt what we are doing with our children and, ultimately, leave us feeling exhausted.

But it's not all bad news. Our new brain is also responsible for many innovations, lifesaving inventions and incredible acts of kindness and empathy, which are helpful to us as parents. Our new brain can comment on, judge, evaluate and question our experiences and emotions. However, this ability can also get us into lots of trouble and lead to self-criticism, fearful imagination, fear of feelings, avoiding emotions, shame and rumination. As parents, we are at the mercy of our biology and genes, which (through no fault of our own) can be very stressful at times.

Our experiences – we are socially shaped

We deal with this issue in more depth in the next chapter, so we will only touch on it briefly here. But, in a nutshell, our experiences shape who we are. We have very little control over the social circumstances of our lives. For example, we did not choose our beliefs, our preferences, our faith, our personality, our families or the culture and societies we live in. So much of who we are is based upon things outside our control.

Imagine you were adopted at birth by a tribe living in the Amazon rainforest. Would you be the same version of yourself sitting here today? The answer is no. You would be different. We don't know what version, but we know it would be different.

Now imagine that you were adopted at birth by your neighbours. Would you be the same version of yourself sitting here today? Again, the answer is no. We do not know what version, but you would be different.

Emotions – why we have them

Unfortunately, society often teaches us that emotions are dangerous. We come to believe that we shouldn't feel anxious. We shouldn't feel angry. We shouldn't feel sad. We hear that we should always feel happy and that our children should also always feel happy. If they are not, then we need to *fix* things. We are told that unless you are happy, there is something wrong.

This is not only unhelpful, it also contributes to our ongoing mental health crisis, as young people inevitably feel a negative emotion about something and then get into a spiral of self-criticism ('I shouldn't feel like this', 'There is something wrong with me'), which in turn leads to feelings of shame. Enough of this can lead to the development of mental health disorders, such as depression (which is not the same as sadness).

Let's have a look at the emotions in more detail, and why we are pre-programmed to experience them:

Emotion	Why these emotions have evolved
Anxiety	Forms part of our threat detection system, which protects us from danger by prompting us to run away, fight or freeze. If we meet a lion, anxiety would drive us to run towards safety
Anger	Another element of our threat detection system, which prompts us to protect ourselves from danger or ensure our survival or status with a show of power. If someone steals all our food, we would display anger as a way of showing our displeasure and to get our food back
Sadness	We are safer as part of a social group. If a group member went missing from the cave, sadness may prompt us to go and look for that person. It may also be part of helping us to rest and rejuvenate when we have been injured

Disgust	Feelings of disgust help us to stay away from things that are potentially poisonous. If you have food poisoning after eating something, that food item usually elicits disgust. This is linked with an evolutionary mechanism prompting us to stay away from something that could make us sick or even kill us
Drive and excitement	This is our human drive to have more and seek out things that increase our chance of survival (e.g. building a house, hunting for food and finding a mate)

Attachment and soothing

Absolutely fundamental to this book is the concept of attachment and its link to our soothing system. For anyone who is interested in this, read the book *Why Love Matters* by Sue Gerhardt. It is a stark reminder of how the lack of a secure, loving attachment to a caregiver impacts on children (and adults).

Mammals (including humans) provide care to their young in many ways, such as through food, shelter, protection, love and affection. Babies use physical cues (e.g. crying) to notify their caregivers that something is not right and to signal that they need their caregiver to take care of the issue (e.g. changing their nappy). In the 1950s, John Bowlby (a psychiatrist and psychoanalyst) conducted ground-breaking research, which found that the quality of our attachment relationships have a huge impact on our lives. Caregivers who were attuned and responsive to the needs of their young were more able to build secure and stable relationships with them, resulting in a secure attachment style. For example, these caregivers provided their children with positive facial expressions, sharing of positive emotions, voice turns, stroking and putting boundaries in place. These elements create a secure and safe haven, which soothe and settle our children. The infants and children whose needs were not met were likely to develop an insecure attachment style, which can cause problems like them having a lack of trust and a fear of intimacy. Secure attachment relationships between an infant/child and their caregiver(s) play an absolutely vital role in buffering children from a variety of physical and mental health issues.

Unfortunately, in our society, attachment to one's caregiver is often seen as a negative thing. How many times have we heard very young children being praised for not showing any emotion when leaving their caregivers to go to unfamiliar adults (e.g. to new nursery workers or supply teachers). Obviously, we want our children to develop feelings of safety and to feel soothed in a care setting, but it is absolutely normal and natural for children to feel apprehensive and unsafe when they are first away from their caregivers.

There is also evidence that our attachment relationships have a significant impact on our soothing system – our ability to soothe and calm ourselves when we feel threatened or are overwhelmed. This system is linked to the production of certain hormones (oxytocin, endorphins and opiates), which help us to feel calm, content and peaceful. There is now evidence that receiving support, affection and care helps us to engage our own soothing system, which in turn has an encouraging effect on our children, enabling them to feel brave enough to explore the world around them.

Thus, by providing a sense of safeness through a secure attachment, our child is able to develop courage. And, as we explained above, this inner courage is very important, as it is a key part of compassion, and helps us face and then accept or manage the difficulties in our lives rather than trying to avoid such difficulties.

So, to summarise, the care and compassion we receive in our attachment relationships help us to develop our soothing system and our courage, which in turn help us to cope with difficult situations and emotions.

Emotion regulation systems

We have learnt about attachment and the soothing system. Now it is time to introduce the idea of the three systems of emotional regulation. This was an idea coined by Paul Gilbert, which he called the emotional regulation systems approach. It is a fundamental part of compassion-focused therapy. The three systems are colour-coded, as shown in the diagram below:

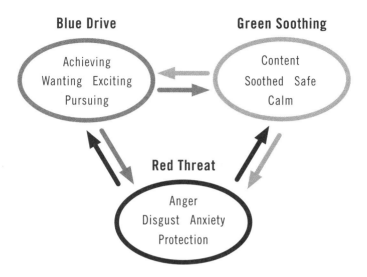

Blue Drive

Achieving
Wanting Exciting
Pursuing

Green Soothing

Content
Soothed Safe
Calm

Red Threat

Anger
Disgust Anxiety
Protection

Adapted from Gilbert, *The Compassionate Mind* (2009) with permission from Little, Brown Book Group Ltd.

The compassion-focused therapy approach explains that we all have:

- a drive system (blue)

- a soothing system (green)

- a threat system (red)

These three systems are in each of us and, when they are balanced, they work to complement one another. So, if the threat system is activated but there is no actual threat (e.g. there isn't a lion nearby), the soothing system helps to calm this response down. Equally, we may be faced with a drive task (e.g. writing an exam), which can cause us stress and anxiety. Our soothing system will then hopefully step in to balance out the anxious feelings.

Problems arise when these three systems are out of balance. For example, too much drive can cause positive emotions to fade with time, while also contributing to a lack of inhibition, along with a continuous desire for more and feelings of never having enough. Such an imbalance can also create addictions. Our modern world is full of drive.

Too much threat system can leave us feeling constantly on edge, full of anxiety and avoidance and with a heightened anger reaction. Many mental health disorders are centred in an overactive threat system. When our soothing system is too small, we may feel unable to regulate and calm ourselves. Unfortunately, people who had traumatic childhoods or who developed insecure attachments with caregivers may experience more difficulties accessing their soothing system. We can see how having an imbalance between the three systems can cause problems in our parenting. For example:

- Too many drives (e.g. multiple clubs to drive children to, job demands to fit in, supporting homework, life admin, meal planning, etc.)

- Too many threats (e.g. tight work deadlines, homework deadlines, lost PE kit, school behaviour points, upset child, etc.)

- Not enough soothing (e.g. no time to relax in the evening, too tired to socialise, no time to yourself, no time to exercise, etc.)

This is where compassion-focused training becomes essential to help us fully understand the interplay between how we have been socially shaped, our tricky brains, how we deal with our emotions and how we balance the demands of our threat, drive and soothing systems.

Evidence-based parenting approaches and compassionate parenting

There is a lot of advice on how to parent out there. Some parenting strategies are what we call 'evidence-based', which means they have research backing up how effective they are. These are the techniques we will be referring to in this book. They suggest different ways to moderate 'problem' behaviour and disobedience, while encouraging children to become more compliant and show more positive behaviour. However, little is known about how these parenting techniques promote other, key aspects of our children's development, such as their considerate behaviour, empathy, kindness and general wellbeing.

This is where compassionate parenting comes in. There is new and exciting research suggesting that parenting characterised by compassion leads to positive outcomes in our children, regardless of the parenting strategy used. In this book, we will be introducing parenting strategies underpinned by evidence and grounded in compassion.

We will now introduce our EASE compassionate parenting model, which we will revisit throughout the book.

The EASE steps to compassionate parenting

Compassionate parenting involves four steps:

- E   **Emotions**
- A   **Actions to soothe**
- S   **Stopping with compassion**
- E   **Emotions now?**

'E' Emotions

The first step in compassionate parenting is to stand back and work out which emotions you are experiencing as a parent, as well as the emotions your child may be feeling, in as non-blaming and accepting a way as possible.

Spotting our own parental emotions

This is essential, as the emotions we experience tell us a lot about what is going on in our minds, which can impact on our parenting. Our emotions tell us:

- How we're thinking (e.g. if you're angry, you're likely to have angry thoughts, such as, 'How dare you!' Whereas, if you're worried, you're likely to have more nervous thoughts, like, 'People are going to think I'm a terrible mum')

- We might be remembering past times that remind us of the situation we're in now (e.g. times in the past when your child refused to eat their dinner now that they are once again refusing to eat it)

- What we do in this moment, which may be different to what we'd ideally like to do

- Our emotions then shape the actions we end up taking – including our parenting actions

As we learnt at the start of this chapter, difficult emotions are normal for us humans. And so, while you might feel calm and collected during a difficult parenting moment with your child, there's every chance that you're also feeling stressed, angry, guilty, fearful and more! As Halle Berry (the actress) said:

*'For me, motherhood is learning about the strengths I didn't know I had
and dealing with the fears I didn't know existed.'*

The commonly known phrase 'knowledge is power' works well for emotions, too. If we have knowledge of the emotions we are feeling in any situation and are aware of what is going on in our minds alongside these emotions, this knowledge gives us the power we need to accept and respond appropriately, in order to help ourselves in the best way possible. However, you have to be open to acknowledging emotions in yourself that might feel uncomfortable, along with their associated impact on your state of mind. For example, it is much easier to admit to feeling and behaving in an excited and cheerful way than it is to admit to feelings of disgust or anger, with the associated thoughts, memories and desires to act in disgusted or angry ways.

This first step of recognising your own emotions also helps to slow down your busy new brain, with all of its reactions that may or may not be helpful in the moment. Instead, this step gives you a minute of quiet in your mind, to work out what you are really feeling and what is going on in your mind.

Spotting our child's emotions

A second key part of the 'E' emotions step is being in tune with the emotions and needs of our children. They may be experiencing just one feeling in a given moment, or they may be having a number of feelings all at the same time. Your child might even have emotions that conflict with one another. For example, feeling delight when enjoying the taste of the extra biscuit they have sneaked out of the family biscuit tin, but also feeling guilt at knowing they have broken a family rule to have a second biscuit.

If you are able to tune in to the emotions your child is feeling, your parenting strategies may be more successful. It could also be helpful to imagine yourself as if you were your child, feeling their feelings at the age they're at – rather than imagining their feelings as the adult you are now. This can make it easier to really understand what is going on for them.

If you notice during the 'E' emotions step that your own emotions are starting to overwhelm you, or they are becoming unhelpful or difficult, particularly in light of your child's own emotions, then you may need to move on to the next step of:

'A' Actions to soothe

The idea of this second step is to help us regulate our emotions to a greater extent, rather than expecting them to disappear completely. This is because we are unable to turn off our emotions at the touch of a light switch. Emotions are connected to our bodies and minds and reflect underlying changes in our physiology, such as the release of various hormones (like adrenalin, endorphins and cortisol), which come with associated biological changes (such as a faster heart rate and headaches). Nevertheless, using soothing actions helps us be in better control of our emotional states, which then puts us in the best possible place to use our compassionate parenting strategies.

The actions to soothe will be unique to each of you. For one person, stroking your pet cat might help you to regulate your emotions once more, whereas, for someone who is allergic to cat fur, this would be much more stressful! The actions to soothe include all the activities you do when you are in your own soothing system.

You may also need to support your child to put some of these actions to soothe in place to help them regulate their own emotions. We will explore both your and your child's tailor-made actions to soothe in the following chapters, to prepare you both for the third step of EASE.

'S' Stopping with compassion

Only during step 3 do we move into the actual parenting strategies, as we generally need to do the E and A steps first in order to be in the right head and body space to parent compassionately. The S strategies vary, depending on which area of parenting you are focused on, but may include:

- Tuning in to your compassionate rather than your critical mind – which has the three strands of wisdom, strength and a commitment to the most healthy way forward, as described earlier

- Using this warm, compassionate approach with your child: speaking with a kinder voice tone, posture and facial expression, even when having to manage difficult parenting moments

- Putting a parenting strategy in place, such as a reward system, a collaborative plan with your child, or natural consequences or compassionate responses to your child's struggles

- Helping your child connect with their own compassionate mind, showing them how to stop with compassion, rather than slipping into a critical mindset themselves

'E' Emotions now?

The final step of the EASE model is to reflect on the outcome of your compassionate parenting, connecting with how your emotions and mind have changed from the start to the end of the parenting episode, how your child's emotions have changed (hopefully, they are in a calmer or more manageable place now), and what you have learnt along the way. It may be at this point that you spot a new, difficult emotion within you (such as guilt or remorse), which signals that the parenting encounter did not go as you planned. This is normal for all of us; despite our best efforts, we sometimes make mistakes. Therefore, standing back and looking once more at our emotions can tell us if we need to do more. Admitting to mistakes and reconnecting with your child is incredibly powerful and can then help ensure that you always finish a parenting moment in a compassionate way.

However, the hope is that, on most occasions, your further examination of your emotions and your child's emotions shows that the more difficult emotions have faded and you have both moved forward in a helpful manner, through the journey of parenting.

We will explore this compassionate parenting approach in more detail over the next six chapters.

In summary

Compassionate parenting begins with these core elements:

- Parenting is hard. There is no one-model-fits-all approach when it comes to parenting

- Evolution has shaped our brains. We did not choose our tricky brains. Humans have a complex connection between their old and new brains

- We are shaped by biology and genes. It is a genetic lottery

- Our experiences, biology and evolution have made us who we are and how we parent. We did NOT choose this

- We all experience a range of emotions. This is part of being human and they are in-built in us and our children

- Our emotions can help us work out what is going on in our mind, such as the thoughts we're having, the memories we might have of similar times, and the parenting actions we want to take

- We need to understand attachment and its connection to the soothing system, and how it develops courage within our children

- We have three emotion regulation systems: drive, threat and soothing systems. In an ideal world, these should be balanced and interact with each other to help a person regulate. This can be very difficult to achieve in the midst of parenting

2 A Compassionate Understanding of Yourself and Your Parenting Approach

All children are born with different physical appearances, different personalities and a unique set of skills and challenges. This is wonderful, as it is every child's uniqueness that makes them truly special.

However, we often have parents who come to our clinic who have parented their older children without any particular difficulties and then suddenly struggle to know how best to parent a younger child, who just doesn't seem to respond to the techniques that worked so effectively with their older children. This can result in parents experiencing a strong inner critical voice that says they are poor parents, unable to parent this more 'difficult' child. They also have other uncomfortable emotions, such as confusion and despair about what to do next.

When experiencing difficult emotions and a sense that you can't effectively parent your child, it is helpful to first step back and explore what it is about the dynamic between the child and you that is bringing up these feelings in yourself. It can also be helpful to think about how you've shaped your vision and developed your knowledge of how to be a parent, which might be further impacting on your emotions, your mind and your subsequent parenting actions. Clinical psychologists call the process of understanding ourselves more deeply 'working out a formulation'. Such a process allows us to map out why we are acting

and feeling as we do (e.g. our past experiences and our genetics), what issues this is causing us (e.g. our associated thoughts, feelings and actions) and why these issues aren't going away.

We are going to explore the formulation of your parenting approach in this chapter to ensure you have full wisdom about yourself as a parent. This knowledge can then help you to take the steps you feel are needed to change your approach to both your child and yourself as a parent.

Your wisdom formulation of you as a parent

Nothing occurs randomly with parenting. In order to know how to adapt and shape our parenting responses, it is helpful to first understand ourselves as parents to a greater extent. We need to look at the combination of:

- The genetics that make you 'you'
- Your past experiences that will shape your approach to parenting, including:

  1. Your experiences of your own parents and/or guardians (and their parenting)

  2. Your experiences of being cared for by people who weren't your parents

  3. Any other life experiences that link to your parenting

1.   Genetics: Your own unique personality

Personality can make a difference to your parenting, as your genetic makeup shapes your approach and response to all of life's experiences – including your interactions with your own children. Therefore, it can be helpful to examine your personality traits, to build up a picture of who you are as a person and, more specifically, how that then impacts on your parenting.

Worksheet 1 will give you a sense of your general personality. But how does this affect your responses as a parent?

Worksheet 1: Your personality

Circle all the personality qualities that fit you best. It is important to be honest with this exercise, circling the qualities you actually have, rather than those you'd like to have:

Assertive	Confident
Anxious	Gregarious
Extroverted	Introverted
Energetic	Relaxed
Perfectionistic	Messy
Laid back	Open
Patient	Impatient
Passionate	Ambitious
Competitive	Stubborn
Intolerant	Creative
Adaptable	Mindful
Other:	Other:

Let's take the example of a seven-year-old girl called Asha, whose favourite pastime is singing the same song lyrics over and over again, throughout all the waking minutes she can manage!

A <u>naturally patient and carefree</u> parent may feel in a soothing state about Asha's singing and is able to ignore this behaviour, allowing Asha to continue to sing whenever she wishes.

Whereas a <u>more impatient parent</u> might feel in a threat state when Asha repeats a song on multiple occasions, experiencing irritation and annoyance, and will have to tell Asha to stop singing or to change the song.

And a <u>gregarious, extrovert parent</u> might feel driven to perform with Asha and feel excited to join in!

We can see how our personalities shape our emotion regulation systems, along with how we might react to our children's behaviour and, in turn, determine what we do next as parents.

2.   Parenting experiences from our own parents and/or caregivers

Throughout your childhood, your parents would have made choices about how to parent you, based on their own personalities and upbringing, which would, in turn, shape your attachment to them. This would naturally have affected your own internal beliefs about what a 'parent' looks like, and how you should act in this parenting role.

It is important to recognise at this stage that the accepted style of parenting has shifted since you were a child and, thus, what was considered acceptable when you were a child may now no longer be acceptable.

For example, smacking children was not unusual as recently as the 1980s and early 1990s, even to the extent of children being left with 'handprints', where their parents had made contact with their skin. However, smacking is no longer viewed as acceptable parenting and is illegal in many countries. Researchers have also found that smacking three-year-olds contributes to these children experiencing poorer mental health as they grow older and developing difficult behaviour patterns. Therefore, if you were smacked when you were younger, it does not mean that you should smack your own children. However, you might have the same urge to give your child a consequence (in a different way) for acting in a manner that would have resulted in you being smacked by your own parents when you were a child.

Let's think back to Paul Gilbert's three emotional regulation systems, which were introduced in Chapter 1, from the perspective of your parents. One of the three systems we discussed was the threat system, which can detect and act upon the potential threats to ourselves and others (both physical and social). Various factors would have triggered your parent's threat system when they were parenting you and these may now influence your own threat system as a parent.

Spend a few minutes thinking back to your childhood and recall which issues triggered your own parent's threat systems – then complete Worksheet 2.

Worksheet 2: Triggers of your parents' and/or key caregivers' threat systems

Tick the factors that triggered your parents' and/or caregivers' threat systems:

Threat factors	Tick/cross	Threat factors	Tick/cross
Family being late		Drug taking	
You (as a child) being late home		Alcohol drinking	
You (as a child) getting lost		Illness in the family	
Injuries		Lack of schoolwork being done	
Work stress		You (as a child) leaving work until the last minute	
Rudeness from you (as a child)		Aggression from you (as a child)	
When you (as a child) didn't follow their instructions		Untidiness	
You (as a child) withdrawing from them		Family finances	
Lack of revision being done		Other:	

We often learn threats from our parents and then adopt the same ones they did. For example, if your parents always experienced stress about whether or not you had completed your homework, repetitively reminding you to complete your homework after school, there is a good chance that you also try to ensure that your children complete their homework in a timely manner and may check up on their progress.

Which of these threats do you share with your own parents and may even struggle with as a parent? Record them in Worksheet 3:

Worksheet 3: List of the threats you share with your parents

Do you have any threats that you don't share with your parents? We can end up acting the opposite to our parents, too. For example, if your parents lived in a very tidy house, it may be that your house is messier than theirs and your threat trigger is hearing other people comment on how to keep homes neat, rather than being triggered when your house becomes untidy. This shows how patterns can be broken and change over time. Jot down any threats you are aware of in yourself that you don't share with your parents in Worksheet 4:

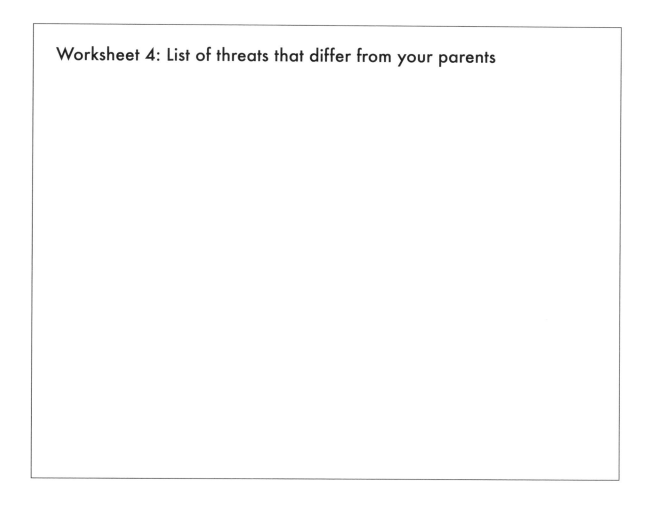

Worksheet 4: List of threats that differ from your parents

What were your parents' and/or caregivers' drive systems like?

As outlined in Chapter 1, we all have a drive (incentive and resource-focused) system that pushes us forward, helping us to achieve our goals and meet our needs. In turn, this drive system allows us to feel positive feelings of excitement and happiness. Think back to a time when your parents were working through a plan (e.g. getting ready for a holiday or day trip, succeeding at work or making their house look as they wished it to). What factors influenced your parents' approach to these tasks? And what activities gave your parents a feeling of pleasure and success?

Look at Worksheet 5 and tick any drive factors and exciting activities you remember your parents having when you were younger:

Worksheet 5: Parents' and/or caregivers' drive system

How they approached drives	Tick/cross	Sources of excitement & positivity	Tick/cross
Organisation/pre-planning		Sporting pursuits	
Time punctual		Competitive activities	
Late/chaotic/rushed		Holidays	
Messy		Work-related activities or feedback	
Doing everything themselves without help		Friendships	
Completer/finisher		Religion	
Perfectionism		Meals out	
Starting but not finishing		Days out	
Delegating tasks to others		Receiving positive feedback from your teachers, coaches or club leaders	
Music		Other:	
Other:		Other:	

Which of these pleasurable activities and ways to approach drives do you share with your parents now you are a parent yourself?

Record them in Worksheet 6:

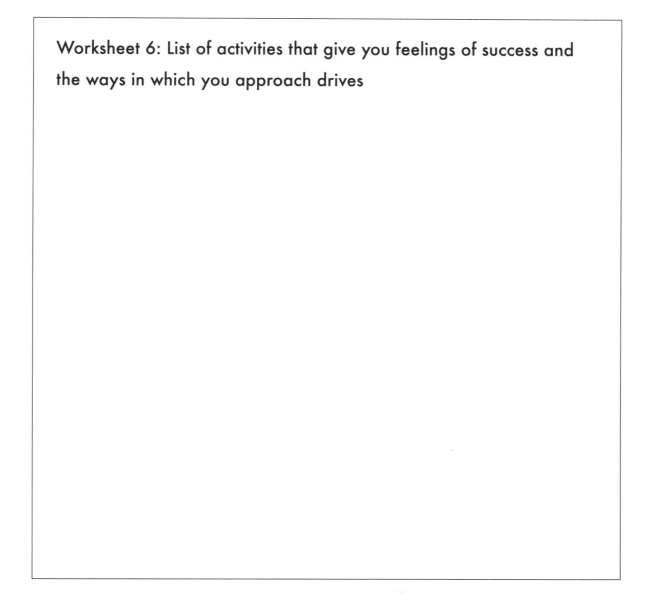

Worksheet 6: List of activities that give you feelings of success and the ways in which you approach drives

What ways did your parents undertake soothing activities

to regulate themselves?

Your parents will have needed to give themselves 'time out' to relax and recover from the demands of their lives, including from parenting; and to calm down after being in a threat state or after a drive activity.

Think back to when you saw your parents at home after work, or at the weekend when you were a child. Also think about what your parents did after an argument or confrontation (with yourselves, with their partners or other people in their lives). Their behaviour may not always be what we would consider healthy. At this stage, it is important to look at them honestly and non-judgementally.

In Worksheet 7, tick the soothing strategies you remember your parents using:

Worksheet 7: Your parents' soothing strategies

Soothing strategy	Tick/cross	Soothing strategy	Tick/cross
Cuddling others		Doing exercise	
Massages		Gardening	
Other types of physical soothing		Listening to music	
Seeking reassurance		Doing a hobby (e.g. sewing, knitting, DIY)	
Going to their bedroom		Playing a game	
Leaving the house		Watching TV	
Chatting to other adults		Drinking alcohol	
Retreating to a quiet space (e.g. study/shed)		Reading	
Taking drugs		Smoking	
Other:		Other:	

Think back to when you were a child and felt upset or distressed. Did you turn to your parents or caregivers for comfort? If so, what did they do next?

Now look at Worksheet 7 and think about how you calm yourself down as an adult when you feel frustrated and, generally, how you look after yourself when you're feeling stressed. Are these soothing strategies like your own parents' strategies, or different? Record them in Worksheet 8:

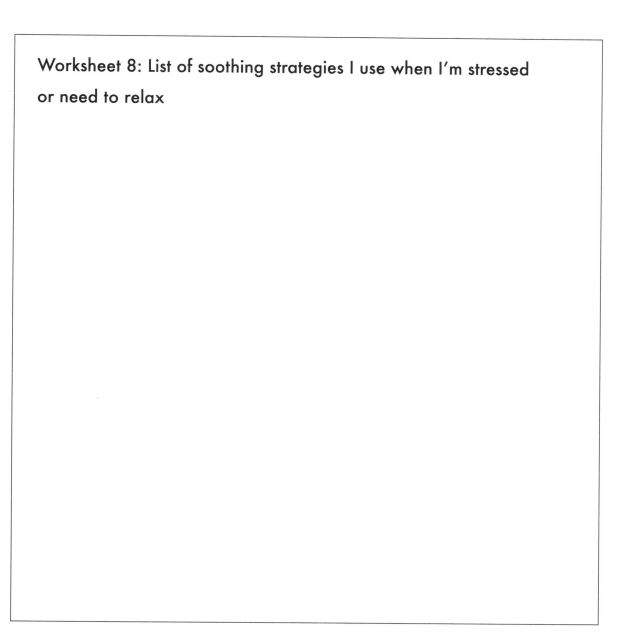

Worksheet 8: List of soothing strategies I use when I'm stressed or need to relax

As you can see, the experiences you had with your own parents have shaped the parent you are today in many ways, including: the triggers for your own parenting stress; the ways you go about achieving parenting (and other) tasks; and how you rest and restore when you need to.

However, it is rare for our childhoods to occur in a 'bubble' in complete isolation from other adult figures, with just our parents as influential caregivers. Other adults may also have a role in shaping who we become as parents. This is because humans are inherently social animals, who have always lived in a 'pack' with other humans, right from our early, nomadic days.

Therefore, it is also important to consider the other adults in your childhood, to explore their impact on the parent you are today.

3.   Parenting experiences received from others

Who were the key caregivers in your life (apart from your parent/s)?

In childhood, we come into contact with many people who have a greater or lesser impact on shaping our sense of how adults should care for and parent children and teenagers. Have a think about the people who were most important in your early life, who are likely to have influenced your sense of how a parent should behave:

Worksheet 9: Key people in my childhood/teen years

Tick to indicate which people from this list were key in your life:

Possible key people	Tick/cross	Possible key people	Tick/cross
Close family members (e.g. aunts/uncles, grandparents)		Extended family members (e.g. great aunts/uncles, cousins)	
Teachers		Older sibling who was a 'parent' figure	
Neighbour		Religious leaders	
Scout/Guide leaders		Other youth group leaders	
Sport coaches		Music teachers	
Friends' parents		Friends' older siblings	
Counsellor/therapist		Other (please specify):	

Look back at the people you identified as having played a role in your life growing up. How did they influence your sense of how a child should be looked after?

Example

Mandy remembered attending church every week and also attending holiday church events. Reverend Johnson, who headed up her church, strongly believed in the importance of the church family – including all the children – coming together before or after a service to share their stories and support each other as necessary. These occasions were always centred around food, such as the church family sharing a simple supper of a jacket potato, soup and a roll, or a bowl of pasta and sauce. Mandy used to love the chance to chat freely with a wide group of children and adults, while enjoying the food being shared.

When Mandy became a parent, she continued a similar tradition with her own family to the one Reverend Johnson had instilled in her; always eating their meals together, with everyone having the opportunity to share their stories of the day and support each other with any challenges they faced.

As you can see from the case of Mandy, she learnt a value about caring for children from her religious leader that she ended up incorporating into her everyday parenting. However, our learning from other adult figures is not always about doing the *same* as they have done but can sometimes be about acting in a different way that feels better.

Example

Ten-year-old Abraham attended a local swimming club with a very strict swimming coach called Kyle. Abraham remembered Kyle as nearly always shouting at him and the other boys in his swim squad, criticising their efforts and telling them that they were not trying hard enough. Despite being an excellent swimmer, Abraham remembered that he often felt demotivated and dreaded his swimming sessions, as he was scared about the comments Kyle would make about him. When he was only ten, Abraham decided that, if he ever worked with children, he would always try to treat them well, and speak to them rather than shout at them, so they enjoyed the activities they were undertaking.

Therefore, the adults in our childhood can make a big difference to us, in terms of both what type of parent we become, and also, the type of parent we don't want to become.

Look back to the adult(s) you identified as important to you in Worksheet 9. Note down the ways they influenced the parent you are today in Worksheet 10 (whether this is because you are doing something similar, or something purposefully different to them):

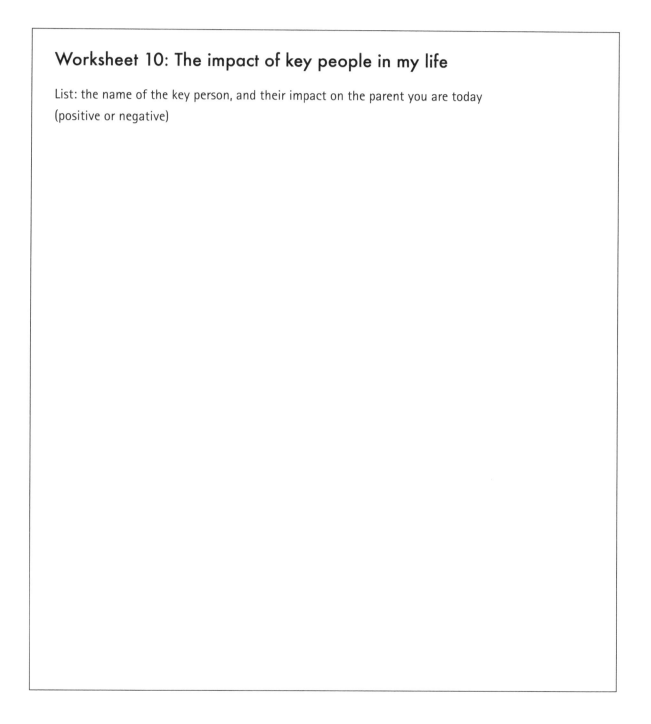

Worksheet 10: The impact of key people in my life

List: the name of the key person, and their impact on the parent you are today (positive or negative)

It is worth noting at this point that our memories can unfortunately have a bias towards remembering negative experiences more strongly than positive ones. This is linked to our brain development, back in our Stone Age days. It was helpful for our new brain to remember negative experiences more vividly to help ensure our survival. For example, remembering our parents' warnings about entering a nearby jungle that was full of wild animals would have been important to protect us from entering that jungle again and risking our lives.

The same process still occurs now. So, you may vividly remember being told off by an adult from your community, or by a parent or caregiver during your childhood, as your new brain is trying to protect you from any recurring dangers. This means that you tend to remember the big scoldings rather than all the times the adults around you were being kind to you.

However, we are a product of our memories, as well as our experiences, and thus our development as a parent may be influenced by these more negative memories as well.

4. Life experiences that link to our parenting

The final area that can shape the parent you become is simply the relevant experiences you have had over the years leading up to and even during your parenting. These experiences can be wide and varied, as everyone's journey through life is different. However, examples might include:

- Learning about parenting strategies through books, TV or online programmes, or more formalised academic courses

- Observing your friends and family becoming parents and witnessing the different parenting choices they make

- The influence of news stories on our approach to parenting. For example, many people were affected by the trauma Madeleine McCann's family went through when she was kidnapped during a family holiday in Portugal, which may have influenced subsequent parenting decisions around child safety in holiday complexes

- Accidents, injuries, illnesses and other conditions that you or others have had can shape your thoughts and approaches to parenting. These can include physical ailments, mental health difficulties, such as anxiety and depression, and conditions such as being deaf, having autism or attention deficit hyperactivity disorder

Spend a few minutes thinking about all the different life experiences you have had over the years that may have influenced your approach to parenting. Jot them down in Worksheet 11:

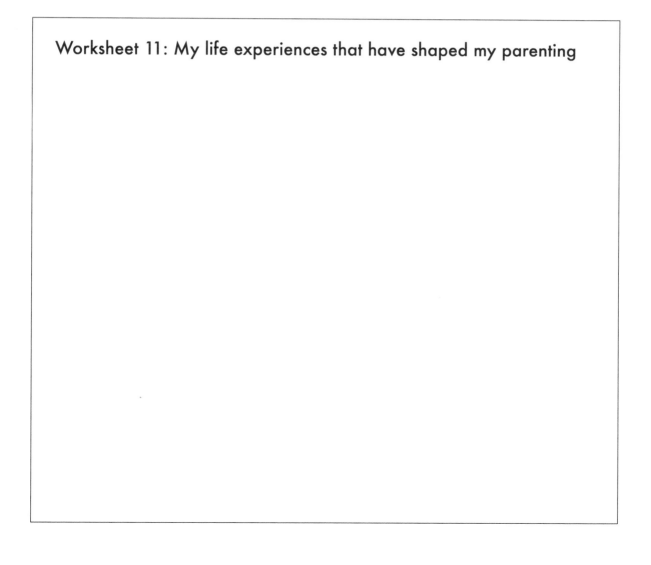

Worksheet 11: My life experiences that have shaped my parenting

As you can see, we do not become the parents we are today by accident. A number of factors are at play, including: our genetics, the parenting we received as a child, the approaches and messages we had from the other adults in our life who had a role in looking after us, and the experiences we had over the years.

It can be helpful to pull all this learning together, to help you see in a simple diagram the influences behind you becoming the parent you are today.

Pulling the formulation together (1)

You can now use all the learning from the worksheets you have completed throughout this chapter to draw up your own personalised parenting formulation.

If you look at the 'Me as a parent' formulation on page 39, you can see six boxes that refer to some of the worksheets you have filled in:

- Genetics/Personality – from Worksheet 1

- Threats – from Worksheets 3 and 4

- Drive – from Worksheet 6

- Soothing strategies – from Worksheet 8

- Impact of key people – from Worksheet 10

- Learning from life experiences – from Worksheet 11

Fill in these boxes on your 'Me as a parent' formulation, but don't complete the other three boxes as yet (in other words, ignore the 'My worries and fears', 'Protective strategies' and 'Unintended consequences' boxes for now).

Hopefully, by looking at your parent formulation, you are starting to get a sense of who you are as a parent, and where your parenting approach has come from.

We now need to consider your **worries and fears**, as these help to explain why your critical mind might be triggered and the reasons you may act in ways that differ from your 'idealised view' of being a parent.

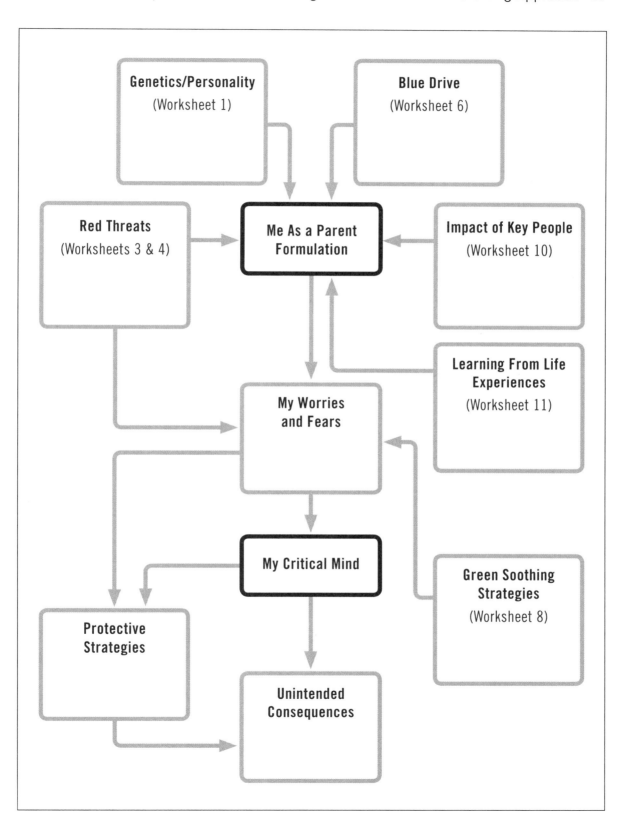

Pulling the formulation together (2): My worries and fears

Let's think of the example of James, a thirty-six-year-old dad of nine- and eleven-year-old boys, and his formulation, to gain a sense of how worries and fears can develop.

James's example: 'Me as a parent' formulation

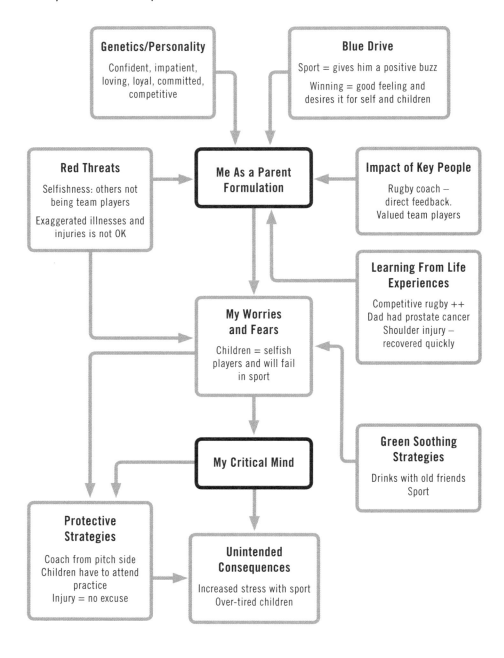

As you can see from James's formulation, his early years playing competitive rugby greatly shaped his view of being a parent. An influential rugby coach helped James to recognise the importance of teamwork, and he always valued the coach's direct approach with him and his other teammates. James's life experiences were key, too, including when he had to support his own father through prostate cancer at an early age and seeing his dad make a full recovery, plus James quickly bouncing back from a nasty shoulder injury, enabling him to play rugby once more.

These experiences, plus James's personality and drive, resulted in him developing threats when he believed people were being selfish (and thus, in his mind, not being full team players) and also when people reported an injury that he did not perceive to be serious. James wanted his two sons to value their sport and to be valued sports players – and this meant a great deal to him as a dad.

James naturally developed **worries and fears** as a parent about his two sons not being fully committed to their football and rugby out-of-school sports teams. These fears were all-encompassing, and included:

- When the boys seemed to be trying to avoid practices at times (e.g. saying, 'I'm too tired for practice today, Dad!' and the more general, 'I don't want to go to training, Dad')

- When he believed his children were not passing the ball to other team members enough

- When they were hurt during a practice and he believed they were exaggerating the pain they were in

Now we will think about your own worries and fears as a parent.

Look back at your 'Me as a parent' formulation. Can you spot any worries and fears that have naturally developed from your early experiences and your personality, and which affect your approach to parenting? These are often your fears about your child's future, or how other people might judge you or them. These fears might include:

Your child being ill or hurt	People thinking you're a bad parent
Your child being bullied	Your child not meeting their potential
Your child becoming rude or a 'bad kid'	Being a 'helicopter' parent
Being too 'soft' a parent	Your child being obsessed with or addicted to something

When you have worked out your parenting worries and fears, add them into your 'Me as a parent' formulation on page 39.

Pulling the formulation together (3): Protective strategies

It is natural to act in ways that protect us from our worries and fears to ensure they do not come true. This is the case for all our worries and fears, for example:

Worries and fears	Protective strategies
A spider might come close	Run away from the spider!
I'll make a fool of myself during a presentation	Let our colleagues do most of the talking
Getting lost on the drive to a holiday resort	Plan the route and use sat nav

As you can see from these examples, some of our protective strategies can be seen as positive and helpful – such as using sat nav on a journey. Whereas other protective strategies might not be what we'd ideally use, but they are still what we fall back on when our worries and fears have been triggered – such as running away from spiders.

The same is true for our parenting worries and fears. These naturally lead us to undertake various strategies that aim to protect us or our children from a negative event or experience.

If we look back at James's formulation, you can see that his protective strategies were to quickly check his sons for injuries and then tell them directly to 'get back onto the pitch' once more. He would also shout from the side of the sports pitch, to remind his sons to pass to their teammates, and would debrief them in the car on the way home after matches, pointing out how they could have improved their play. James also took his sons to every match and training session, whatever the weather – unless they were genuinely unwell (above the level of a cold).

Have a look at your 'Me as a parent' worries and fears. What protective strategies do you use to help you cope with and manage your parenting fears? Again, it is important to be honest about these strategies; some may be the type that you could feel positive about (e.g. James encouraging his children to attend sports practices, whatever the weather), and others may feel less desirable (e.g. James shouting at his children from the sidelines). These less desirable strategies are often the ones that our critical mind focuses on, so we need to be truthful to ourselves about them, in order to help us develop a more compassionate mind.

Once you have identified your protective strategies, write them into your 'Me as a parent' formulation on page 39.

Pulling the formulation together (4): Unintended consequences

As mentioned earlier, our protective strategies are not always as helpful or positive as we want them to be and this can result in unintended consequences.

For example, James recognised that shouting from the sidelines at football and rugby matches irritated the coaches and sometimes embarrassed his two sons. His nine-year-old son had also expressed the wish to stop football, which had led to numerous arguments about whether he was allowed to quit or not, which had put a strain on their relationship. James also recognised that sport was becoming the only topic of conversation at home, which was taking the fun out of family life. Plus, his sons were feeling increased pressure to perform well at all sports matches.

James's critical mind was well aware of these unintended consequences. He started to experience self-criticism about being a 'bad dad for causing the stress within the family' and had the sense that he had 'failed' to make his sons the sporting successes he'd hoped for.

Look back at the protective strategies you identified in the 'Me as a parent' formulation. Can you recognise any unintended consequences that may have occurred as a result of these strategies? Would your critical mind give you a tough time about these unintended consequences?

Add the unintended consequences section into the 'Me as a parent' formulation on page 39.

You have now worked through the whole formulation to gain a greater understanding of your approach to parenting, the reasons this approach developed and some of the challenges you may face because of the strategies you have adopted over the years, including potentially triggering your critical mind. In the following chapters, we will explore how you can use this knowledge to develop a more compassionate mind towards yourself as a parent, and also how to understand and develop compassion within your child.

In summary

It can be helpful to develop a formulation of 'Me as a parent', looking at:

- Our genetics and personality

- Experiences from our own parents or carers, including emotional regulation, states of threat, drive and soothing

- Experiences from other adults in our earlier lives

- Other life experiences that link to our parenting

- Our parenting worries and fears that subsequently develop

- The protective strategies we adopt in light of our worries and fears

- The unintended consequences of these protective strategies

- The fact that our critical mind can link up with this formulation

3 Compassion for Yourself

As we discussed at the start of this book, parenting is hard. It would be a lot easier if we were handed a tailor-made manual along with our babies when they were first born, so we would know exactly what to do with our unique child and ensure a smooth parenting journey. What often seems to happen instead is that we are forever criticising and questioning ourselves – feeling guilty about everything we do or don't do correctly as parents.

This guilt is *normal* and everyone experiences it. Having a whole variety of other difficult feelings and experiences is also normal, but it is all too easy to feel as if it's only you who is somehow 'doing it wrong' in your parenting. In fact, this self-criticism about our parenting is universally experienced but is rarely discussed.

In this chapter, we will look at the reasons behind this guilt and self-criticism and consider how we can develop a kinder approach to ourselves when we parent our children, with all their strongly held thoughts, feelings and desires.

It is important to remember that parenting is like helping your child to build their own house. The goal is for them to build strong houses, from which they can go off into the world, feeling safe, secure and confident. However, parents are part of the foundations of these houses and, thus, we want to help ensure these foundations are as strong as possible, so our children can, in turn, build a strong house on top, to cope with everyday life.

The biology of parenting

It is helpful to remember the difference between our old brain and our new brain . . .

The old brain

As explained in Chapter 1, the old brain holds our emotions, behaviours and motives:

- Emotions: such as fear and guilt about getting things wrong and pride when parenting goes well

- Behaviours: including our fight-or-flight response

- Motives: our intentions, including being caring, avoiding harm and becoming competitive ('the best parent ever')

The new brain

Within our new brain, we have an image of ourselves as a parent that we have built up over all the years of our life. This may be based on our own parent's approach to parenting, stories we have read, or observing friends and family becoming parents. However, the new brain likes to have an idealistic view of our parenting.

Thus, while our new brain may give us energy for activities such as 'baby planning' (e.g. setting up the best nursery furniture we can find before our baby is born, or picking out the perfect buggy), it can also cause us to ruminate about what we have done wrong in our parenting.

The new brain's ability to think about our thinking can lead us to self-criticism and self-doubt as a parent:

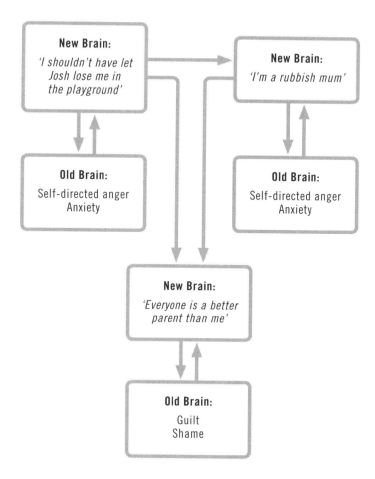

You can see how the new brain can quickly trigger self-criticism and how the old brain contributes to the negative emotions we feel about this criticism.

Parental critical mind

Everyone has an in-built self-critic in their mind. This is a normal human experience and is generally linked to an underlying intention we have, which may not necessarily be negative.

Examples of the parental critical mind

'I screwed up again trying to help my daughter with her spelling'

'It's my fault that my son keeps having tantrums'

'I'm the worst mum here'

This self-critic generally makes us feel negative about our own parenting and doesn't always help us:

Example

Mary is a mum of six-year-old Jake and ten-year-old Sophie. Mary struggles to get out of the house on time for the school run and finds herself rushing around up until the last moment, often shouting at Jake and Sophie to hurry up, and nearly always leaving the house five minutes later than she intended to.

What was Mary's situation?

Being late to leave for school once more.

Links to the past:

When she was younger, Mary's own parents were never late for any event and would regularly discuss the importance of being on time for activities.

What was the intention of Mary's critical mind?

To ensure Mary left for school on time, hoping that this would reduce Mary's stress levels.

What Mary's critical mind said when she was late:

'You're such an idiot. You never get out on time. The school is going to think you are such a bad mother for always bringing Jake and Sophie into school late, particularly as their names will be in the late book again.'

How Mary felt after her critical mind spoke:

More stressed, hopeless, embarrassed and ashamed.

As you can see from Mary's example, she ended up feeling worse after her self-critic spoke, and this stress, embarrassment, shame and hopelessness may well affect Mary for the next few hours of her day and into the following morning, when she tries to leave the house once more.

Think of a time you can remember when your own self-critic was telling you that you had parented badly. This may be similar to Mary, when you're late for an event. You may have other reasons, such as when you've lost your temper with your child or parented in a way that did not fit into your new brain's ideal or the times when your child behaved in a way that you may blame yourself for. Then complete Worksheet 12:

Worksheet 12: My critical mind

What was the situation?

Links to the past:

(e.g. from your own parenting, or past experiences with other people, or different situations)

What was the intention of your critical mind?

(e.g. to make yourself feel bad, to prevent an issue from happening, or to help you in some way?)

What your critical mind said:

(try to use the actual words, which can often be harsher than what you would say out loud, including swearing to yourself)

How you felt after your critical mind spoke:

There is always a cost with the critical mind, despite it sometimes having positive intentions (like in Mary's case, trying to prevent her from being late). The problem with the critical mind is that it has unintended negative consequences, such as gradually decreasing our confidence, our happiness and even our enjoyment of parenting. It can also lead us to feel exhausted, stressed and low.

Our critical minds often have patterns in what they say or the areas they focus on. In Mary's case, her self-critic was loudest around timekeeping. However, many other themes, often linked to our parenting worries and fears, can trigger our critical mind, which you may have become more aware of as you completed the 'Me as a parent' formulation in Chapter 2.

Parenting is tough enough

As we outlined at the start of this chapter, parenting is an incredibly tough job. Adding to the challenge, some of us already receive feedback from the people around us about whether or not we are doing a 'good' job as parents. We do not need any additional criticism about our parenting, especially from ourselves, as we know the words to use that will hurt and upset us and cause the most negative consequences.

Therefore, building a COMPASSIONATE APPROACH TO YOURSELF about your own parenting is an invaluable skill to learn.

Parental compassionate mind

The first point to note about being more compassionate to yourself is the fact that you can't ignore the intentions of the critical mind, as these intentions will have driven you to being self-critical in the first place.

For example, in our earlier case study, Mary would not believe her compassionate mind if it said: 'It doesn't matter if you're late. Relax. Who cares?'

This is because Mary's upbringing strongly reinforced the importance of being on time for events (including school). Therefore, she would not believe such a compassionate message to herself and would quickly disregard it, probably shifting back into the more familiar critical mind.

The second issue is that our critical mind is usually triggered when we are feeling emotional ourselves and are thus not in a calm state in both our bodies and our minds. As we all know, it can be incredibly difficult to change how we act when we are feeling a tricky emotion and, as we have seen, human biology prevents us from doing so.

Therefore, to be an effective parent, it is important that we initially recognise the **emotions** we are feeling, to know whether or not to connect with our compassionate mind. Then, we can take **actions to soothe** ourselves, to make it easier to distance ourselves from our critical mind, by **stopping with compassion**. We can then re-examine our **emotions**, to see if this has been helpful for us. This brings us back to:

The EASE steps to compassionate parenting

We can follow four steps to strive towards compassionate parenting:

E   **Emotions**

A   **Actions to soothe**

S   **Stopping with compassion**

E   **Emotions now?**

'E' Emotions

The critical mind is a little bit like an old friend, in that it has been with you for many years, coming and going with no effort on your part. This makes it hard to spot its presence but without being aware that the critical mind has been triggered, you are unable to take a different approach to it.

This is where our emotions can help us.

Example

Martin is a dedicated dad of three children: Molly, Sarah and Billy. He works long hours and is often out of the house before his children are up and returns home after they've had their dinner. Nevertheless, Martin tries to be home to help with the bedtime routine and have some quality time with his children. However, on many week nights, they are tired after school and become 'silly' at bedtime – not following his instructions and using every tactic they can think of to get out of bed once more.

One evening, Martin is desperate to flop on the sofa and relax after a hard day at work. He loses his temper and shouts at the children, telling them how bad they're being. This makes Molly and Billy cry. Martin then feels guilty and upset, as his parenting critical mind tells him:

'I'm bad with the children. They've not seen me all day and I've just been really angry with them. Why am I so bad at parenting? My wife is so much better than I am. What's the point of coming home early for bedtime when I go and screw it up?'

Martin may not be aware that his critical mind has spoken, or that memories of other times when he has lost his temper have flashed into his brain, adding strength to his critical inner voice. But he will notice feeling sad and guilty about losing his temper with his three children. These difficult emotions therefore give Martin clues that his critical mind had been triggered and are a signal to him that he could try the EASE strategy.

Multiple feelings

You might notice that Martin experienced a couple of different emotions after losing his temper. He was feeling guilty AND upset (and probably still a bit angry too, as this emotion can take time to fade away). We often feel more than one emotion in one moment and the cocktail of the emotions can increase their impact.

For example, when dropping your child off at primary school for the first time, it would be understandable to feel any / all of these emotions:

Sadness	Anxiety	Excitement	Pride	Guilt
E.g. as it represents the 'end of an era' of being with your child all the time	E.g. in case your child doesn't settle or enjoy school	E.g. such as having more time to yourself and excitement for your child	E.g. often around the sense of your child growing up (and how they look in their uniform!)	E.g. guilty feelings because of your excitement to return to the 'world of adults' once more

In this example, it might be that the parent experiences all of these emotions at the same time, or that they move through sadness, to anxiety, to excitement, to pride, to guilt and then back to sadness again within a few minutes. As outlined in Chapter 1, these emotions are all *normal* and having them is part of being human.

Depending on our children's behaviour, we may find that one of our three emotional regulation systems are triggered. It might be that a child triggers our soothing system and we therefore want to comfort and cuddle them. But it could also be that our children's behaviour activates our threat or drive systems, which can lead to an increase in our parental worries and fears. Then, our protective strategies are triggered, which may have unintended negative consequences.

Therefore, it is good to be aware of the emotions you are experiencing in the moment, as this gives you opportunities to help yourself and be ready for your critical mind to kick in.

Being mindful of our emotions

How do you know when you are happy?

What are the signs that you are angry?

What do you do when you are sad?

Emotions are part of our biology and thus we all express them through our bodies, as they affect what we want to do, what we end up doing, what we think, what we remember and what we feel.

Example

If you bring to mind a professional footballer who has just scored an all-important goal, they typically run around the side of the pitch, smiling, dancing, jumping – and sometimes even doing gymnastics moves!

What are the signs that YOU are feeling difficult emotions, that might have been triggered by your critical mind? You might find it easier to spot your emotions by how your body feels. Or you might notice them more because of the types of thoughts you have while feeling them. Alternatively, it may be that you are more of an 'action person' and 'act first, think later'. Then your behaviours might be the best sign of your underlying feelings.

Complete Worksheet 13 to explore the signs you've noticed that indicate you are feeling a particular difficult emotion.

Worksheet 13: Signs of my emotions

ANXIETY/FEAR

Body signs:

(e.g. racing heart, butterflies, fidgety, fast breathing)

Anxious thoughts:

(e.g. I can't do that; this is too hard)

Actions:

(e.g. pacing, running away from the danger, avoiding something scary)

ANGER

Body signs:

(e.g. racing heart, feeling hot, making fists, scowling)

EMBARRASSMENT

Body signs:

(e.g. blushing, racing heart, butterflies)

Embarrassed thoughts:

(e.g. I can't believe that just happened. Someone might have seen me)

Actions:

(e.g. hiding your face, moving away, making yourself 'smaller')

SHAME

Body signs:

(e.g. feeling empty, feeling sick)

Angry thoughts:

(e.g. That was out of order. How dare they do that)

Actions:

(e.g. shouting, moving fast and determinedly, slamming doors)

Shame-based thoughts:

(e.g. I'm the worst parent ever. I've messed up my kids. It's all my fault)

Actions:

(e.g. crying, hiding away, wanting to hurt oneself)

SADNESS

Body signs:

(e.g. tearful, emptiness)

Sad thoughts:

(e.g. It's too much for me. This is so awful)

Actions:

(e.g. crying, seeking comfort, giving up)

OTHER EMOTIONS (that feel important to you)

Body signs:

Thoughts:

Actions:

The aim of the 'E' (emotion) in EASE is not to change the emotions you are feeling in the moment. But to instead recognise them and accept and understand why they have cropped up – particularly when the critical mind has been unkind to you about some of your parenting.

Knowing the 'E' also helps you understand what is going on in your mind generally, such as why you are having memories of similar times or wanting to act in certain ways (even when you know these actions aren't always the 'best' in that moment).

Recognising the 'E' then allows you to take care of yourself through rallying your compassionate mind. However, this is very difficult to do when we are feeling intense emotions, and thus we often need to act first to soothe our bodies and minds.

'A' Actions to soothe

The 'A' in EASE is the next step in the process, which is us undertaking a soothing action when we are experiencing a difficult emotion, in order to get our minds and bodies into a place where we are 'ready to receive' our kinder inner voice.

There are many ways to sooth our systems. These can be:

- Individual and unique ways to calm ourselves down
- Breathing strategies
- Cheerleading ourselves

Individual ways to calm ourselves down

We all have our own unique ways that help us de-stress when we are feeling emotional; whether that is making a cup of tea, splashing water on our faces, walking in the garden, phoning a friend or stroking a pet.

Look back to Chapter 2, Worksheet 6, where you listed the ways in which you calm yourself down. Which one or two might you be able to use when you are feeling difficult emotions and need to reduce the intensity of these emotions in order to best hear your kinder, compassionate mind?

My calming strategies to try when I need to use my compassionate mind:

Breathing strategies

Although breathing is something we all do and is automatic, the way we breathe has a big impact on our bodies. For example, if we breathe quickly, we may start to feel lightheaded and dizzy. Professionals from all walks of life learn breathing techniques as a way of improving their performance. For example, singers learn how to breathe in ways that help them to project their voice. Learning how to slow down your breathing can have a powerful effect on the body and mind. Research has shown that we can activate our soothing system by practising certain breathing strategies, body postures and facial expressions. Here is a soothing breathing rhythm script for you to follow:

Soothing breathing rhythm

Find a quiet place to sit. Take a moment to embody a confident, grounded and open body posture, with your feet on the floor at shoulder-width apart, spine upright and shoulders slightly back and chest open. Bring your head into an upright position and gently bring a friendly expression to your face. When you feel ready, bring your attention to your breathing in a mindful way. Notice the sensations that are present as you breathe in and out, and when your attention begins to wander, gently notice this and bring it back to your breath in a kind and gentle way.

As you are gently holding your attention in the flow of your breath, see if you can find a soothing or calming breathing rhythm. Take some time to experiment with this – explore whether you can slow down your breathing or breathe a little deeper than usual. Find a rhythm that feels comfortable to your body. If you can, try to breathe in a smooth, even way, like a pendulum. If you notice your attention moving away from your breath, or you become distracted in any way, gently bring your attention back to your breath and tune back in to the calming and soothing quality of your breathing rhythm. Spend a minute practising your soothing breathing rhythm.

See if you can imagine a sense of slowing down in your body as you breathe out. It can also be helpful to notice your body feeling a little heavier as you breathe out, while your legs are supported by the chair and your feet are grounded on the floor. Continue practising this breathing rhythm for another five minutes or so, mindfully noticing when your awareness is distracted from this focus and gently bringing your attention back to rest in the flow of your soothing breathing rhythm.

See if you can slow your breathing down a little further. Sometimes it can be worth counting with your breath to start with. For example, try breathing in to a count of five, with each count representing a second. Once you've got to five, hold for one second before breathing out for five seconds (again counting as you do so). Hold for a count of one before breathing in again to the count of five:

In breath 1-2-3-4-5

Hold 1

Out breath 1-2-3-4-5

Hold 1

In breath 1-2-3-4-5

Adapted with permission from *The Compassionate Mind Workbook* by Chris Irons and Elaine Beaumont

People often assume that learning these techniques should be quick and take immediate effect. But learning a new skill takes time and the same is true for breathing strategies. We need to practise them. Start by trying to practise this once a day and see if you can gradually increase the time you spend on these exercises.

Cheerleading ourselves

Imagine that you are an athlete about to compete at the Olympic Games and you hear a crowd roaring their support for you. How do you think that would motivate you in your event? Do you think you'd want to push yourself a little bit more in front of the crowd to achieve the best performance you can?

High-achieving sports men and women often talk about the power of hearing positive messages from the crowd while competing.

For example, Dina Asher-Smith, silver medallist at the European Indoor Athletics Championships, reported to UK Sport in 2015:

> *'There's no better feeling than racing in front of a home crowd and hearing their cheers can really inspire you. I'm so excited to compete in the UK this year and hopefully use that support to give some strong performances and put myself in the best possible position ahead of Rio next summer.'*

When you are having a difficult parenting moment, and your tricky emotions and mind have been triggered, it's unlikely that there will be a crowd of people around you who can cheer you on to 1) manage the moment and 2) be kind to yourself while you do it. And we're pretty sure you wouldn't want a crowd watching you anyway!

However, we *can* cheerlead ourselves through our difficult moments, without the need for others.

Example

At the start of a difficult parenting moment	During a difficult parenting moment	After a difficult parenting moment
E.g. 'Here we go . . . but I know I can stay calm and collected' 'I've got this. I can stay in control' 'I know these moments are tough, but I'm ready'	E.g. 'Keep breathing' 'I CAN stay calm. It's always OK in the end' 'I'm doing the best I can. It might feel the same as last time, but it really isn't as I'm much more in control'	E.g. 'That was really tough but I got through it' 'I need to look after myself for a moment. I'll go and take five to feel better'

What cheerleading phrases could you use that might help to calm your intense, difficult emotions and mind in a tough situation? Complete Worksheet 14 to pull together some ideas:

Worksheet 14: My cheerleading phrases

Think about times when you've felt as if you were struggling while parenting, which may have then triggered your critical mind. Are there any cheerleading phrases you could have used that might have helped you to gain more control over these feelings? List your ideas in the table:

At the start of a difficult parenting moment	During a difficult parenting moment	After a difficult parenting moment

Now you know which 'E' emotions are triggered in difficult parenting situations and which 'A' actions will help you to gain more control in readiness to fight your critical mind. It is now possible to aim for a more compassionate approach to your own parenting.

'S' Stopping with compassion

The next part of the EASE strategy is to connect with your compassionate mind to support and help with parenting.

We base this compassionate mind on the three core aspects that were outlined in Chapter 1:

1.   Wisdom – to understand ourselves and our children

2.   Strength – to face into difficult emotions and situations rather than avoiding them

3.   The caring commitment – to alleviate distress in a way that is helpful and not harmful

Take Mary's example:

Example

Mary's wisdom: Her wisdom recognised how important it was to her to be on time. It also noted other factors in play, such as the fact that Jake and Sophie had eaten a leisurely breakfast that morning, which had contributed to the lateness. Plus, Mary had needed to do a few extra 'jobs' before school, which had eaten into the time. In addition, while typically leaving the house five or ten minutes late, Mary's wisdom connected with past memories of school mornings and the fact that Jake and Sophie were actually rarely late to school; she normally got them into the playground just in time.

Mary's strength: Rather than slip into her usual pattern of criticising her own lateness, Mary could dig deep and connect with her inner strength to be more kind to herself, and also maintain strength to deal with any repercussions for being late, if any.

Mary's caring commitment: Mary was exhausted from feeling stressed about lateness each morning and thus felt it was OK to be more caring towards herself about this. This, in turn, would help reduce Jake and Sophie's stress (as they didn't like it when their mum became stressed and started shouting at them to hurry up).

Therefore, Mary used her compassionate mind to tell herself:

'Goodness, school mornings can be stressful and it does seem hard to leave the house with enough time to get Jake and Sophie to school on time. However, I seem to just about get them to school OK most mornings, so hopefully this will be one of those mornings. I will take two deep breaths, as I'm feeling quite stressed. Then I will try my best to get out of the house in the next minute, calmly. And perhaps I can set my alarm clock to wake me up five minutes earlier tomorrow. I've got this. Come on, me!'

How do you think Mary would feel if she said this to herself?

Would it have an effect on the time she left the house? Is there a chance she would end up leaving earlier, as she would be calmer and more able to think clearly about getting out the house on time?

Compassionate tone of voice

We all know how we can interpret text messages differently, depending on the tone of voice we use to read them. For example, if we receive the message:

'Are you sure you're all right?'

We could interpret it as:

- Caring – if we read it with a kind voice in mind, or

- Irritated – if we read it with a sarcastic voice in mind

Thank goodness for emojis, which help give context to our messages!

This tone-of-voice issue is also important with our parenting compassionate mind. When our self-critic has been triggered, it is very easy to speak to ourselves in a cross, frustrated, stressed or mean voice – even if we are, theoretically, using kinder words to ourselves – which causes the compassionate message to be lost. Therefore, when thinking about striving towards compassion in relation to our parenting, it is important that you use a compassionate, kind, supportive tone of voice when speaking to yourself (out loud or in your head). We will explore this in more detail in Chapter 5.

If you're not sure how to speak to yourself in a kind way, it can be helpful to copy someone you know, who always takes a gentle and kind approach to life. You can do this in Worksheet 15:

Worksheet 15: A kind person in your life

Spend a minute thinking of someone in your life – past or present – who speaks to you in a caring way. Try to imagine the words they use with you, the tone of their voice and even their facial expressions and body postures when chatting to you. It may help to close your eyes to do this exercise, as this can bring more detail. You can then jot down some of the things you notice:

The types of words they use:

The types of words they don't use:

Their tone of voice:

Their facial expressions:

Their body positions:

Hold this in mind, as this is the compassionate approach you are going for. It will include how you speak and also how you hold your body and your facial expressions.

Do facial expressions really matter?

Yes! Try this mini facial expressions experiment:

Facial expressions experiment

First, say to yourself, 'Hang in there, you can do this!' while frowning or scowling. What happens to your voice tone? How much do you believe the words?

Now repeat, 'Hang in there, you can do this!' with a softer, more neutral expression. How did this feel? How much do you believe the words now?

As you can see, it's helpful to try to move towards a softer, neutral facial expression when speaking to ourselves, as it can really change the message we are trying to give.

Your compassionate mind

Think of a time when your self-critic was triggered about some aspect of your parenting. You might want to choose the example you focused on in Worksheet 12, or another example that feels like the right one to focus on first. Now complete Exercise 1:

Exercise 1: Connecting with your compassionate mind

Start by shifting your breathing to a more rhythmic pattern – this means slowly breathing in for the same amount of time as you slowly breathe out (e.g. breathing in for three or four seconds, then out for three or four seconds)

Connect with your compassionate tone of voice, neutral facial expression and relaxed body position

Then think about:

- the wisdom of the situation – for example, the intentions of the critical mind, but also your knowledge of the full picture of what's going on and everyone's roles in it, including the fact that no parent is perfect or the 'ideal parent' we dream about becoming

- Your strength – to do something differently and to fight the critical mind's view of your parenting

- Your caring commitment – as you deserve to feel OK as a parent. You are trying your best and nobody is perfect. Therefore, it is all right to be kind to yourself too

Then allow yourself to be compassionate about the parenting situation you are thinking about and connect with this different way of speaking to yourself in your own mind

Jot down what your compassionate mind said to you:

How do you feel about what your kind voice said to you?

Look back at Chapter 2, when you used your own wisdom to work out the 'Me as a parent' formulation, to identify times when your self-critic might be triggered when you are experiencing parental worries and fears. Which critical mind areas would you like to focus on first, to try to take a more compassionate approach? Jot these down in Worksheet 16:

Worksheet 16: Times to try out my compassionate mind

1.

2.

3.

4.

'E' Emotions now?

The last part of the EASE strategy is to reflect on what you've just done, and the impact of your compassionate mind on your feelings and actions.

We often find that our compassionate mind can ease the difficult emotions we feel when our critical mind is around, while still meeting the self-critic's intentions about what we should be doing.

Look back to your discoveries from Exercise 1, after connecting with your compassionate mind. Were your feelings the same or different to the ones the critical mind gave you? Which inner voice seems more helpful to you: the voice of the critical or the compassionate mind?

Challenges to having a compassionate mind

It can be hard to shift from having a self-critical approach to a more self-compassionate one towards our own parenting if the critical mind has been around for many years. However, the more you practise, the easier it becomes.

Preparation can make life an awful lot easier when first trying to connect with your inner compassionate mind.

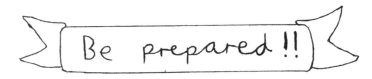

Look at the list in Worksheet 16 then use the guidance in Exercise 1 with these examples to prepare a script to say to yourself, using your compassionate mind in readiness for the situation.

It can be helpful to jot down what you've prepared, so you can remember it in the moment, when your emotions are running high and it is harder to be compassionate. You could note them down:

- On your mobile (in the notes section, or even as a screen saver)

- In an email or message to yourself

- On a sticky note on the fridge door

- Written on your hand

- Anywhere else that makes sense to you

Sometimes, it's too hard to remember to be kind to ourselves in the moment. If this happens to you, it is OK to reflect on the difficult moment afterwards, and take a more compassionate approach then, as it is still good practice. And the more you practise, the easier it becomes to eventually remember your compassionate mind during tricky parenting moments.

In summary

Parenting is tough. Our parental critical mind, which is unique to each person, is easily triggered. It always has some intention behind it (often a positive one) but it can also cause us difficult emotions. We can start to build up our parental compassionate mind through using the EASE strategy, to:

- Work out our emotions and associated tricky mind in a difficult parenting moment

- Undertake actions to help us self-soothe (e.g. breathing exercises, cheerleading ourselves, or our own tailor-made strategies)

- Stop with compassion – using our compassionate voice, with a kind tone of voice and a neutral facial expression to help us find an alternative way forward based on our wisdom, strength and commitment to looking after ourselves in a healthier manner

- Reflect on how our emotions have changed after using our compassionate mind

- Accept it can be challenging to start using a compassionate mind in our parenting and thus be prepared to do so whenever we can

4 A Compassionate Understanding of Your Child

In our previous chapters, we explored the origins of compassion, how to understand yourself better in the context of compassion (our wisdom) and how to begin to make changes to support yourself to make parenting changes (our strength). In this section, we will begin to explore how you can develop your compassionate mind in relation to your child and, by doing this, how you may be able to support any struggles they, or you, may be having.

Many parenting books jump straight in to the strategies and solutions you could adopt to solve the difficulties you may be having. We have so many parents coming to see us who are exhausted, overwhelmed and despondent after trying many of these strategies with limited success.

You may now have an idea of your own critical mind and protective strategies in relation to your own life as a parent. We will now move on to understanding and applying these concepts to your child.

To start with, we would like you to consider your hopes and fears for your child. You may want to spend a moment and engage with your soothing breathing rhythm before carrying out this exercise (see script on page 119). Once you have done this, we would like you to write down three hopes for your child and three fears in Worksheet 17. This is something we will come back to later in the book:

Worksheet 17: Hopes and fears for your child

Hopes	Fears
1.	1.
2.	2.
3.	3.
4.	4.

We have already discussed the complex interaction between your life experiences, how you were parented as a child, and how these influence your own parenting experience. Now, we are going to consider your child in more detail and their unique strengths and struggles.

Your child's formulation

As mentioned in the previous chapter, clinical psychologists call the process of understanding your child's struggles 'working out a formulation'. This allows us to map out why your child is acting and feeing as they are (e.g. from their past experiences and genetics), including their critical mind and what may be keeping these struggles going.

We are going to explore your child's formulation in this chapter, in order to develop wisdom about your child's struggles. This knowledge can then enable you to take the steps you feel are needed, to change your approach to supporting your child (discussed in Chapters 5 and 6).

To understand the difficulties your child is experiencing, we recommend that you use something called the ICEBERG approach:

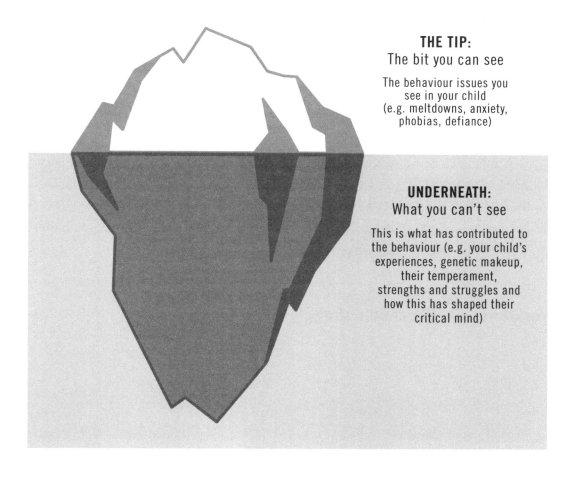

THE TIP:
The bit you can see

The behaviour issues you see in your child (e.g. meltdowns, anxiety, phobias, defiance)

UNDERNEATH:
What you can't see

This is what has contributed to the behaviour (e.g. your child's experiences, genetic makeup, their temperament, strengths and struggles and how this has shaped their critical mind)

What you see – THE TIP

The behaviour your child is displaying is likely to be the reason you were drawn to this book. We want to acknowledge these struggles and consider the impact they are having on your child's and your own life.

Here is a list of common problems in childhood and adolescence, but this is by no means everything.

Common problems in childhood and adolescence

Feeling anxious

Delay in milestones

Difficulties with friends and/or peers

Being bullied

Low self-esteem

Negative self-talk

Feeling low

Meltdowns

Aggression

Self-harm

Phobias (fears of particular things)

Difficulties with schoolwork or homework

Feeling overwhelmed

Withdrawal

Addiction (gaming, alcohol, drugs)

Risky behaviour

Trauma

Defiance

Refusal to engage in everyday tasks

Suicidal thoughts

Backchat

We would now like you to note down the struggles you believe your child is facing at this current time in Worksheet 18. We know it can be hard to put these things into words but try to be as honest as possible. This is not a reflection on your role as a parent, but is rather about naming what your child is struggling with:

Worksheet 18: My child's struggles

As discussed in the previous chapter, it is likely that your child's struggles are having a major impact upon you as a parent. The saying, 'You're only as happy as your unhappiest child,' is relevant here. Being parents ourselves, we understand how your child's struggles may worry you immensely. We understand how exhausting it can also be to support your child with these struggles, especially when you have your own struggles and pressures yourself.

We would like you to take a moment to think about how your child's struggles affect you and note them down in Worksheet 19:

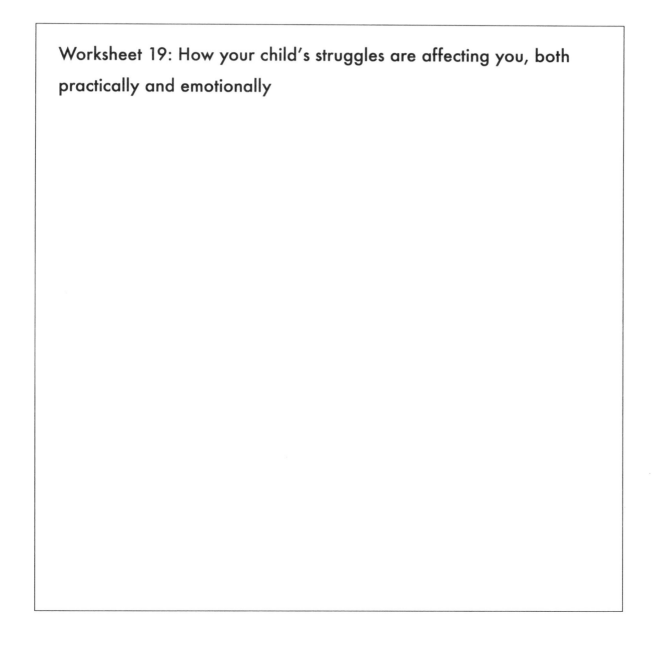

Worksheet 19: How your child's struggles are affecting you, both practically and emotionally

Hopefully, in Chapter 3, you had time to think about how to support yourself through this with your parental compassionate mind. We recommend returning to Chapter 3 from time to time to check in and make sure you are fostering your compassionate mind. This will help you support your child to develop their own compassionate mind.

What lies beneath – UNDERNEATH

We now would like you to consider what may lie beneath the behaviours or emotions you see in your child, by focusing on these three areas:

1. Genetics and experiences

2. The three emotion regulation systems

3. Your child's critical mind

1. Genetics and experiences

We now want you to consider what may be *underneath* your child's struggles – the part of the iceberg you cannot see. Remember, this is not about blame, but about understanding *why* your child is struggling. This WISDOM will be the key to being able to support them in the future and helping them to foster a compassionate mind.

We want you to start to consider what may have shaped your child, from their genetics and biology to their experiences in the world. To help you to build up your child's formulation, look at the following questions and example:

Infancy

- What kind of temperament did your child have as a baby? (e.g. settled, unsettled, curious, relaxed)

- Was it easy to form a bond with your child when they were born or was this more difficult?

- Did your child feed well or did they struggle to feed?

- Were they sociable or more reserved?

- Did your child experience any issues with reflux or colic in infancy?

- Did they have any health issues in infancy?

- Did your child have a learning disability that affected them in infancy?

Example

Tao was born a few weeks premature and spent some time in special care separated from his parents. This made it difficult for his mother, Julie, to breastfeed him. When Tao came home from hospital, he was very unsettled and experienced silent reflux, which was only discovered later. Being a new mother, Julie was often told that 'it's normal', even though she felt that things were not normal. Tao struggled to sleep and was awake every hour. Julie found it hard to manage the sleep deprivation and found herself experiencing some low moods. At times, Julie found it was hard to settle Tao and did not know how to comfort him.

Toddlerhood and early childhood

- Did they have the 'typical' meltdowns or were these more intense?

- Were they strong-minded or easily distracted/diverted?

- Did they reach their milestones at a typical age (e.g. talking, walking, social interaction)?

- Did they settle at nursery/pre-school after a little while, or did they find separation very hard?

- How did they sleep? Were they often hard to settle?

Example

Tao was late to speak. He struggled to communicate what he was feeling, which tended to come out as meltdowns. These happened frequently, both at home and at pre-school, leaving his parents exhausted. They struggled to understand the triggers for the meltdowns and Tao continued to struggle to communicate his feelings and wishes to others. Tao also struggled to nap, which left him emotionally fraught later in the day.

Middle childhood

- How did your child experience school?

- Did they find academic work easy or challenging?

- Did your child have any learning issues that played a role during this period?

- Were they diagnosed with any conditions during middle childhood, such as ADHD, autism, or a physical health issue (such as needing to wear grommets or having Type 1 diabetes)?

- How did your child get on socially? Did they find it easy to make friends and fit in, or was this harder for them?

- How did your child cope when things did not go their way?

- Did your child experience any bullying?

- Did any major life events (parental separation, bereavement, moving home) occur during this time?

- What was your child's relationship like with the adults around them (parents, teachers)?

- Did your child experience any potentially traumatic events, big or seemingly small?

Example

Tao went on to settle at Reception, but had some issues with other children, particularly when they did not follow the rules. He was naturally bright and often found other children quite immature, leaving him isolated at times. Tao lost his grandmother when he was six years old, which led to some fears about the death of others who were close to him. He had a difficult experience when a teacher shouted at him for correcting another child's incorrect answer. After this, Tao was reluctant to put his hand up in class. Tao started gymnastics, showing some natural ability. His coach encouraged Tao and he began to excel in this area, taking part in competitive gymnastics.

Adolescence

- What was your child's experience of adolescence?

- Did they go through puberty early or later?

- How did your child cope with the transition to senior school?

- Did they attend a mainstream secondary school, or access an alternative education provision?

- Did your child experience any learning issues?

- Did they gain any diagnoses at this point in their lives, such as ADHD, autism or a mental health difficulty?

- Did they have any general health issues?

- What were their friendships like?

- How did they get on socially?

- Were there any traumatic events or major life events at this time?

- What was their behaviour like during this time?

Example

Tao continued to excel academically but found the transition to senior school hard from a social perspective. He struggled to make new friends and it took him a while to settle. Aged thirteen, Tao experienced some bullying from male peers and he began to ruminate about what others thought of him.

Tao's parents were able to consider the areas that had influenced who Tao is today, including his important experiences, temperament and other relevant information. They noted down some thoughts:

Example

Tao had a difficult start to life and was often in pain from his reflux. It was difficult to soothe him and he struggled to sleep and settle.

Tao found it hard to communicate his needs and wishes when he was young, which often left him feeling frustrated and possibly unheard by others.

Tao was more sensitive than his friends.

He struggled to regulate his emotions and was frequently tired as a younger child.

Tao's experiences of teachers left him feeling unheard.

He was encouraged and supported by his gym coach.

Tao was bullied by boys at school. This has affected his confidence.

We would now like you to write down any relevant information in Worksheet 20 (use the example questions, if they are helpful):

Worksheet 20: My child's experiences, temperament and relevant information

2. The three emotion regulation systems

In the second chapter, you considered what has influenced your three systems (drive, threat and soothing) as a parent and a person. Now we are going to consider what feeds each of your child's three systems.

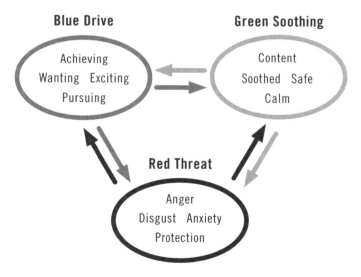

Adapted from Gilbert, *The Compassionate Mind* (2009) with permission from Little, Brown Book Group Ltd.

We do this to recognise all the 'balls' our child is juggling and what activates each system. Remember that these systems all interact. So what activates your child's drive system could also activate their threat system and vice versa.

Drive

To begin with, we would like you to consider times when your child's drive system is activated. This is the system that is incentive/resource-focused, doing things and achieving things. It includes emotions such as excitement, vitality and motivation. Tick the examples in Worksheet 21 that apply to your child:

Worksheet 21: Times when your child's drive system is activated

Drive factors	Tick/cross	Drive factors	Tick/cross
Outdoor sports club (football)		Indoor sport club (e.g. basketball)	
School		Another club	
Homework		Winning games	
Tests		Gaming	
Scoring a goal		Doing a cartwheel	
Other:		Other:	

Threat

Now we would like you to consider what activates your child's threat system. This is our 'threat-focused', safety-seeking system. It includes emotions such as anger, anxiety and disgust. Tick the examples in Worksheet 22 that apply to your child:

Worksheet 22: Times when your child's threat system is activated

Threat factors	Tick/cross	Threat factors	Tick/cross
Being late		Getting sick	
School		Others getting sick	
Getting lost		Tests	
Injuries		Being around unfamiliar people	
Homework		Gaming	
People shouting		Changes to routine	
Sports		Being told off	
Getting things wrong		Untidiness	
Sensory overload		Other:	

Soothing

Finally, we would like you to consider what activates your child's soothing system. This system is associated with feeling content, safe, soothed and connected. Tick the examples in Worksheet 23 that apply to your child:

Worksheet 23: Times when your child's soothing system is activated

Soothing strategy	Tick/cross	Soothing strategy	Tick/cross
Cuddles		Other physical soothing	
Massages		Tickles	
Soft toy or blanket		Reassurance	
Holidays		Distraction (TV, social media)	
Colouring		Being in a safe place	
Gaming		Reading	
Talking about a special interest of theirs		Bouncing on a trampoline	
Chatting to friends		Other:	

Remember Chapter 2 when you considered the strategies your parents used to soothe you. Which soothing approaches do you use as a parent to soothe your own children? Are they similar to those your own parents used or different? Record them in Worksheet 24:

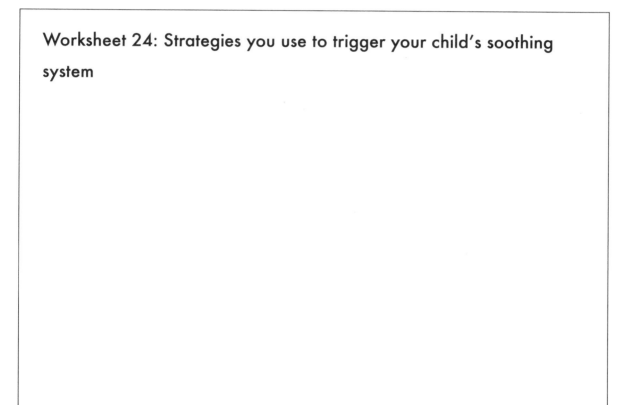

Worksheet 24: Strategies you use to trigger your child's soothing system

You may have noticed an overlap in the items you have written in the three systems. For example, schoolwork could be in both drive and threat; exercise could be in both drive and soothing. Gaming could be initially soothing, but if played for too long or if it does not go well, it could become a threat. Or, if your child is attempting a challenging level on a game or is part of a difficult fighting game with other people, gaming could easily be more of a drive than a soothing activity. The three systems all interact, either increasing or decreasing the others.

When our three systems are balanced, this signals times when we are more regulated. When these three systems are unbalanced, this can cause problems for us and our children.

Example

Billie is nine years old and has begun to have regular meltdowns. Billie's parents considered all the aspects of Billie's life that may feed into her three systems and hypothesised how large or small each system was. As you can see, Billie's threat and drive system were larger than her soothing system. She was part of a theatre group and went to a quite demanding prep school. Billie had barely any downtime or time to regulate and she was having frequent meltdowns and displaying anxiety at the prospect of going to school and to clubs. Billie's mother sat down and used diagrams to show Billie's three systems, thinking about how large or small each of them was. She added what triggered these three systems to the diagrams:

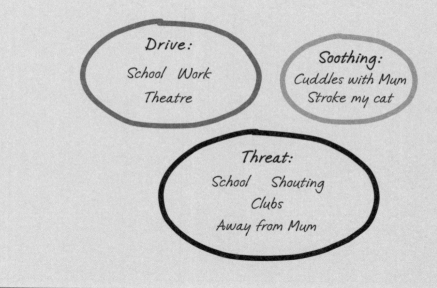

We would like you to take a moment to draw your child's three systems and how large or small they are at this point in time in Worksheet 25. You can collate all the information from the earlier tables to consider what may be activating each of the systems and slot these into the diagram. It can be helpful to use different coloured pens for the three systems:

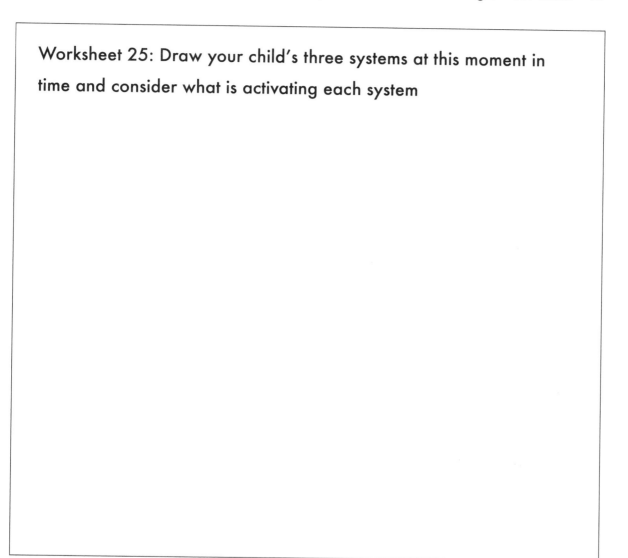

Worksheet 25: Draw your child's three systems at this moment in time and consider what is activating each system

3.   Your child's critical mind

As mentioned, we all have a critical mind. The critical mind often houses our inner fears and worries. For example, your child's critical mind may tell them they're not good enough or make them fearful by telling them that others will hurt or leave them. Your child's critical mind may also be critical about others, saying things like, 'Mum doesn't understand' or 'Dad always blames me.' Remember that the critical mind is formed from our genetics, our experiences and how these have shaped us. This is not about blame or shame, but about wisely considering what may have contributed to your child's critical mind.

We know that your child's critical mind has formed from their experiences and is there to *try* to keep them safe. But it does not always get it right and can get quite nasty and unhelpful in the process.

Often a young person may voice their critical mind during times of distress (e.g. 'I am rubbish', 'I have no friends'). At other times, their critical mind may be more hidden and you may need to hypothesise what it might say to your child. Let's take the example of Tao, mentioned earlier, who is now fifteen years old. After working through the exercises, his mother was able to hypothesise Tao's critical mind, based upon his temperament and experiences. This is detailed in the following example:

Example

Your child – their genetics, temperament and experiences	Your child's critical mind (self, other and the world)
* *Tao was premature, spending time in special care*	* *'I am rubbish at everything'*
* *Tao experienced reflux and was in pain during his early years*	* *'No one understands me'*
* *Tao was a higher-need baby and toddler compared to others*	* *No one can help me'*
* *Tao's mother found it hard to bond with him at times*	* *'I am no good'*
* *Tao experienced speech and language delays in early childhood*	* *'I am unlikeable'*
* *Tao struggled to manage his emotions*	* *'The world is a dangerous place'*
* *Tao struggled socially*	
* *Tao experienced bullying when he was thirteen*	
* *Potentially traumatic experience of a teacher shouting at him for offering another explanation*	
* *Social anxiety*	

We would now like you to spend a moment creating your own understanding of your child. Look back at Worksheet 20 where you noted down your child's temperament and experiences and any other relevant information. Based upon this and your current knowledge of them and their struggles, what do you think your child's critical mind is saying to them? What fears has your child developed over the course of their life about themselves, about others and the world? These are not necessarily 'true', but rather reflect how their critical mind perceives things to be. Note these down in Worksheet 26:

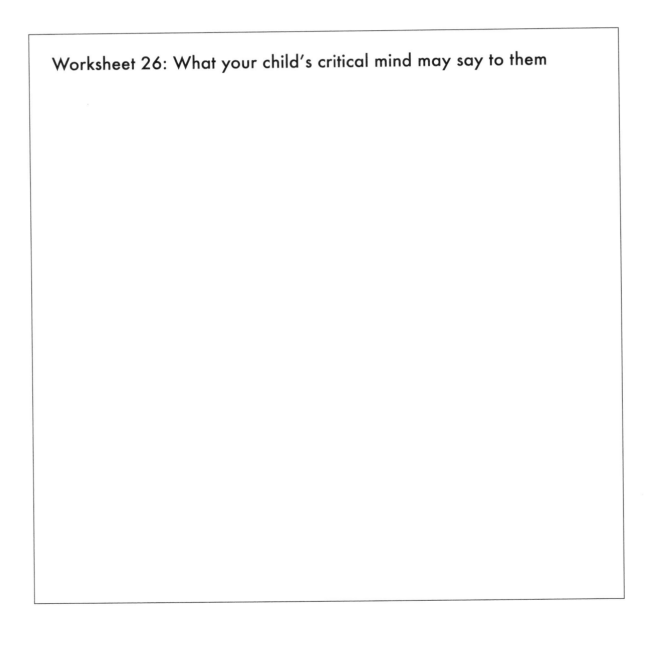

Worksheet 26: What your child's critical mind may say to them

Bringing the tip and the underneath together – protective strategies

We now want to consider how the underneath (genetics, experiences, temperament and critical mind) have impacted upon the tip (the behaviour you see). Think about the possible protective strategies your child has formed to cope with their critical mind. For example:

- If someone fears that they are 'no good', they may give up or avoid tasks as a way of protecting themselves from this fear. Or they may push people away

- If your child has a fear that the world is a dangerous place, then they may avoid going out or they could become hypervigilant and aggressive towards others

- If a young person has autism, they've struggled to make friends over the years and received bullying comments from others that they are 'weird' and 'odd', then they may feel that it is impossible for them to have friends. They may avoid school whenever possible and choose to sit on their own during breaktimes in a library or other quiet settings, away from others

- If your child believes that they are always treated unfairly, they may stop trying new activities as they expect it won't go well for them. Or they may quickly shift to arguing to try to get their needs met

These, then, are, the strategies your child has developed to cope.

Some protective strategies can be helpful for a while but become less effective at a later stage. For example, if school life has become unbearable for your child and they start to avoid school, this may initially reduce their anxiety and help other people realise they are struggling.

However, if their avoidance continues, then your child may be unable to access any educational settings or vocations in the future. They may also miss the opportunity to find like-minded friends and struggle to develop positive friendships.

When thinking about protective strategies, it is important to step back and think about them in a non-judgemental way. It is also helpful to really get into the mind of your child, trying to connect with their experiences as if you were the age your child is, rather than as your adult self. Why would your child be engaging in this behaviour? How is this linked with their critical mind?

We are *not* suggesting that protective strategies (e.g. avoiding school) are necessarily helpful or wise. We are simply trying to understand why they are occurring. By understanding these strategies better, we will then be able to find a wise approach to helping our children, rather than merely reacting to their behaviour.

Example

Alfie is eight years old. He has become increasingly anxious about going to school and cries, shouts and runs away from his parents when they try to get him to go. On a few occasions, his mum and dad have carried him into the car and then handed him over to his teacher, as he cries and screams. Once in school, Alfie is withdrawn and socially isolated. He told his mum that other kids call him names, such as 'stupid' and 'fat'. He also complained that his teacher often shouts in class and says that he does not always understand the work.

We can see that Alfie is really struggling. He is showing high levels of anxiety and is on the verge of avoiding school altogether. Alfie's parents are clearly exhausted and fraught with anxiety about getting Alfie into school. However, they managed to step back and consider Alfie's critical mind and protective strategies. They noted them down:

Alfie's experiences and temperament	Alfie's critical mind	Alfie's protective strategies
Alfie is a sensitive child	*'I am weird and different'*	*Avoiding school*
Alfie has always struggled socially	*'I don't fit in'*	*Running away*
Alfie has experienced bullying from peers	*'I am fat'*	*Screaming at parents to make them listen*
Teacher shouting	*'I am unlikeable'*	*Withdrawing from other children*
Carrying Alfie into school crying and screaming	*'School is unsafe'*	
	'Adults do not listen to me'	

We would now like you to consider the protective strategies you believe your child may be using as a way of coping with their critical mind. Note them down in Worksheet 27:

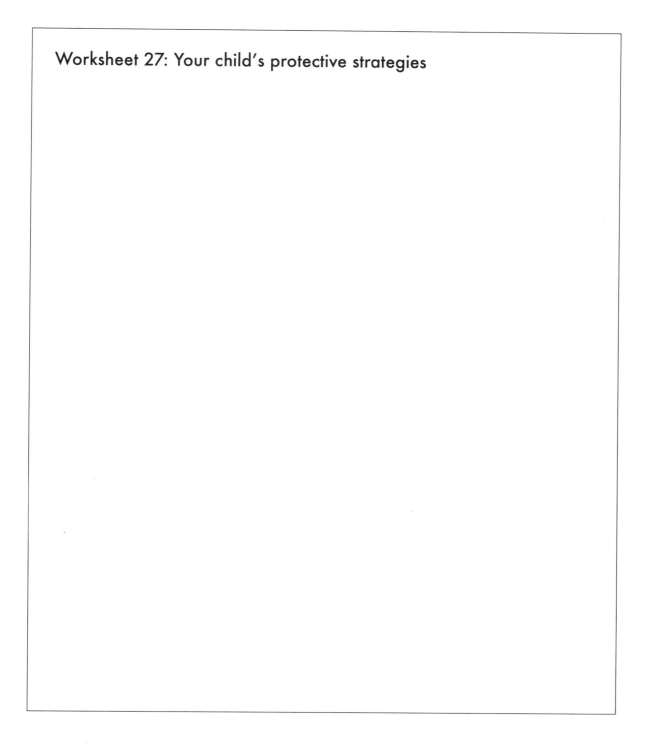

Worksheet 27: Your child's protective strategies

The unintended consequences of these protective strategies

Protective strategies can sometimes appear to help in one context or a point in time, but then become less helpful. They are ultimately there to *protect* your child but are not always wise or helpful.

At this point, we want to consider all the unintended consequences that these protective strategies have for your child. For example, if they are pushing people away, due to their critical mind telling them they will be 'abandoned' or are 'unlikeable', then a possible unintended consequence is that they may become socially isolated and feel even more unlikeable or abandoned.

Example

Let's take the example of Alfie again and his protective strategies of avoiding and withdrawing. His parents were able to consider some possible positives and negatives of Alfie's protective strategies:

Protective strategy	Positives of using this strategy for Alfie	Negative effects of this strategy for Alfie
Running away	*It reduces Alfie's anxiety in the short term*	*Alfie becomes more socially isolated*
Avoiding school	*Teachers may make changes and stop any name calling or bullying*	*Parents and teachers focus on the avoidance rather than the core issue*
Withdrawing from peers		*Alfie misses out on school and falls further behind*
Screaming at parents		*Relationships with parents and classmates become strained and difficult*

Now we would like you to do the same for your child and note down the positives and negatives of their protective strategies in Worksheet 28. It is likely that when doing this exercise, you will notice an overlap between the fears you noted down for your child (mentioned at the beginning of this chapter) and the negative effects of this strategy. It is also possible that you may feel upset, anxious or sad for your child. You may feel angry when thinking about the effect their protective strategies are having upon them. It is OK to experience a range of emotions; you are only human and you care deeply for your child. Remember, in order to work towards a more helpful, compassionate way forward, we often need to walk towards difficult emotions. This is hard, so draw on your strategies to engage your soothing system before and after this exercise:

Worksheet 28: Negative and positive effects of your child's protective strategies

Protective strategy	Positives of using this strategy for your child	Negative effects of this strategy for your child

Bringing it all together

We will now bring all the information together to create a formulation of your child's struggles, just as you did for your own formulation in Chapter 2.

You can use all of the learning from the worksheets you have completed throughout this chapter to complete your own, personalised formulation of your child. Let's take the example of Alfie to show a completed formulation.

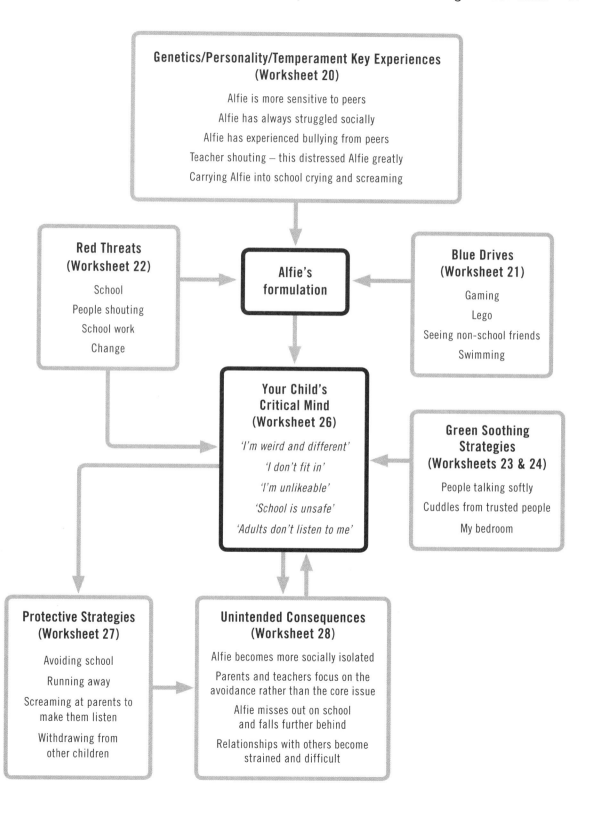

Genetics/Personality/Temperament Key Experiences (Worksheet 20)

Alfie is more sensitive to peers

Alfie has always struggled socially

Alfie has experienced bullying from peers

Teacher shouting – this distressed Alfie greatly

Carrying Alfie into school crying and screaming

Red Threats (Worksheet 22)

School

People shouting

School work

Change

Alfie's formulation

Blue Drives (Worksheet 21)

Gaming

Lego

Seeing non-school friends

Swimming

Your Child's Critical Mind (Worksheet 26)

'I'm weird and different'

'I don't fit in'

'I'm unlikeable'

'School is unsafe'

'Adults don't listen to me'

Green Soothing Strategies (Worksheets 23 & 24)

People talking softly

Cuddles from trusted people

My bedroom

Protective Strategies (Worksheet 27)

Avoiding school

Running away

Screaming at parents to make them listen

Withdrawing from other children

Unintended Consequences (Worksheet 28)

Alfie becomes more socially isolated

Parents and teachers focus on the avoidance rather than the core issue

Alfie misses out on school and falls further behind

Relationships with others become strained and difficult

Take a look at the diagram on page 99. You can see seven boxes that refer to some of the worksheets you have filled in:

- Genetics/personality/temperament/key experiences – from Worksheet 20

- Drives – from Worksheet 21

- Threats – from Worksheet 22

- Soothing strategies – from Worksheet 23 and 24

- Protective strategies – from Worksheet 27

- Unintended consequences – from Worksheet 28

- Fill in these boxes on your child's formulation in the diagram on page 99:

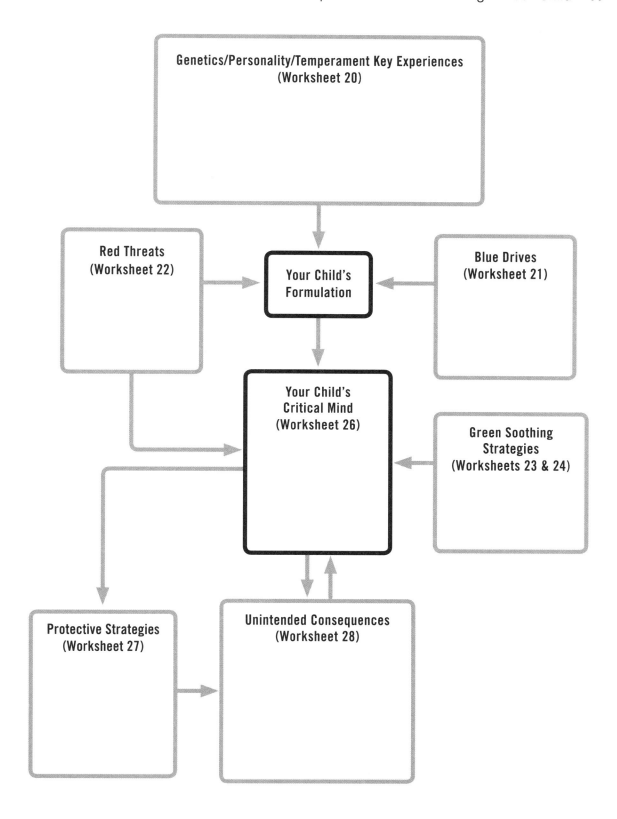

You now have developed a good understanding of your child's struggles and what may have contributed to these and what may keep them going. You have developed wisdom in relation to your child. Remember a formulation is a hypothesis and can be added to and amended at any time. The formulation will aid and support you in the next chapter, which is where we will begin to explore parenting strategies and how to apply these COMPASSIONATELY.

In summary

It can be helpful to develop a formulation of your child, looking at:

- Your child's genetics and personality

- What activates your child's emotional regulation – states of threat, drive and soothing

- Experiences that have shaped their lives

- The formation of their critical mind

- The protective strategies they have adopted to cope with their critical mind

- The unintended consequences of these protective strategies

5 Compassionate Parenting Strategies

Rather than simply jumping straight into various parenting strategies you could adopt, we have asked you in the previous chapter to consider your child's struggles in the context of their experiences and genetics. This is to help you to build WISDOM about the situation they and you find yourself in. This has likely meant that you have had to face some difficult emotions in yourself as a parent, so that ultimately you can support both yourself and your child.

We now move towards compassionate parenting strategies themselves, which you can use to manage your child's problematic behaviour, within a compassionate framework.

A compassionate parenting approach can also be very protective for our children. We, of course, don't plan to shout at our children or lose our temper with them, but parenting can be challenging at times when we are being triggered for whatever reason (e.g. if we are overtired, are already in a threat state, etc.). However, we know that if we can still show warmth to our children, even in the toughest times, then our children are more likely to develop positive wellbeing and learn compassion themselves as adults. There is incredible power in talking to your child with warmth and kindness during moments when the natural instinct would be to shout or tell them off.

The basis of compassionate parenting is to:

- Support your child to recognise and cope with their own emotions
- Find ways of helping them to activate their soothing system
- Use parenting strategies compassionately to manage their struggles

We can follow four steps to move towards supporting and managing your child's struggles, which can be remembered by the acronym of EASE:

- • E **Emotions**

- • A **Actions to soothe**

- • S **Stopping with compassion**

- • E **Emotions now?**

'E' Emotions

As we have already discussed, it is normal to experience a range of emotions. In fact it is an essential part of being a human.

So, we want to consider the range of emotions your child is experiencing and how these emotions then shape their thoughts, memories, bodies and actions. We also want to face into these emotions, rather than avoid them, because they are part of what it means to be human. Russ Harris wrote a wonderful book called *The Happiness Trap*, which highlights how our constant striving for happiness has, in fact, led to a mental health crisis. As discussed in the earlier chapters, emotions are hard-wired into us as humans and we are meant to experience a range of these. In fact, taking away emotions is harmful. For example, if my child isn't worried about a test, then they won't do any revision. By recognising all the emotions we experience, we can start to address them.

In Chapter 3, we asked you to think about the range of feelings you experienced when your child started school. Let's now consider the feelings your child may have had when leaving you for the first time (to go to a childminder, pre-school or when starting school for the first time, for example).

Example

Sadness	Anxiety	Excitement	Pride	Anger
E.g. as they are spending less time with you or at their previous setting. Loss of previous friendships	E.g. about being in a new setting, having a new teacher or carer, meeting new people	E.g. about making new friends, learning new things and starting fun activities	E.g. about being grown up and starting a new 'big' school or doing new things	E.g. about having to leave you or about doing something new, feeling forced to make change

So we can see here how your child will likely experience lots of different feelings about starting school or nursery. This is OK. One emotion may be stronger than another, but ultimately it is important to recognise that we can feel both excited and anxious, sad and happy in a situation. It is also worth remembering that your child may or may not *show* all these emotions. Think of an onion, which has many layers. The outer layer is the emotion your child shows, but beneath this layer are many other layers of emotion. Just because they do not show them does not mean they are absent.

It is also important to be aware of the emotions your child is experiencing in the moment, as this gives you opportunities to support them. Be mindful of how your child's emotions activate your own in various ways. If we want to help our children at times of high emotion, it can be worth trying to activate our own soothing system, so we can remain as calm as possible. This is discussed in Chapter 3. For example, when your child is angry and shouting at you, the natural response may be to become angry and shout back. If you can remain calm, this frees you up to be able to help your child to a greater extent.

As mentioned in Chapter 2, it can be helpful for us to build up awareness of how we experience emotions in our bodies and in our minds. The same is true for our children. We want to support them to recognise how they experience emotions and when they are feeling them. Some children are naturally good at doing this, while others find it hard to notice what they are feeling and when. And this can be particularly challenging for some children who are autistic.

Remember worksheet 13 in Chapter 3, pages 55–6, which highlighted common emotions and how we experience them in the body, brain (thoughts) and what we do (actions). We could consider these emotions through the following example:

Example

Maddy is thirteen and has a diagnosis of ADHD. She is often in trouble at school for talking in class or getting up from her seat. At home, Maddie loves gaming. She has many friends online. She can spend many hours online gaming with her friends. However, this means that she misses homework deadlines and it is often a real struggle to get her to stop gaming. Recently, Maddie had a big argument with her father, following a suspension at school for kicking her friend, Kai, after he teased her about her hair. As a consequence, Maddie's father said she was not allowed to play online for a week.

Here is an example of how Maddie may experience different emotions in relation to this experience:

Anxiety/fear	**Embarrassment**
<u>Body signs:</u>	<u>Body signs:</u>
Racing heart, butterflies, fidgety, fast breathing	Blushing, racing heart, butterflies
<u>Anxious thoughts:</u>	<u>Embarrassed thoughts:</u>
I won't be able to talk to my friends. They may think I don't like them	I can't believe I've been suspended. What will people think?
<u>Actions:</u>	<u>Actions:</u>
Hiding herself under her duvet, refusing to go downstairs	Not making eye contact with parents and teachers, making excuses for her actions, blaming other people
Anger	**Sadness**
<u>Body signs:</u>	<u>Body signs:</u>
Racing heart, feeling hot, making fists, scowling	Tearful, emptiness
<u>Angry thoughts:</u>	<u>Sad thoughts:</u>
I can't believe Kai did that. How dare they take my games away. It's not fair	This is so awful. Life is rubbish
<u>Actions:</u>	<u>Actions:</u>
Shouting 'I hate you' to her parents, moving fast and with determination, slamming doors	Crying, hiding, pleading

As you can see, Maddie has many feelings about this situation. By recognising these non-judgementally, we are able to start to consider Maddie's perspective and can build the foundations to support her in noticing her various emotion states. That does not mean we will always agree or condone the behaviour that comes with emotions, but we can acknowledge how she is feeling and how hard this may be.

Consider something your child is struggling with. For example, are they finding it hard to attend an extra-curricular club? Are they struggling to leave their gaming consoles? Do they struggle with friendships or when situations do not go as planned? Narrow this struggle down and consider a recent example. We would like you to consider the range of emotions your child may have experienced about this situation. If they have not acted on that emotion, consider what that *part* of them wanted to do. Note down your thoughts in Worksheet 29:

Worksheet 29: The emotions your child experiences in different situations

Anxiety/fear	Embarrassment
<u>Body signs:</u>	<u>Body signs:</u>
<u>Anxious thoughts:</u>	<u>Embarrassed thoughts:</u>
<u>Actions:</u>	<u>Actions:</u>

Anger	Sadness
Body signs:	Body signs:
Angry thoughts:	Sad thoughts:
Actions:	Actions:
Shame	Other emotions
Body signs:	Body signs:
Shame-based thoughts:	Thoughts:
Actions:	Actions:

It is now helpful to start to acknowledge these emotions and the situations that led to them. Be curious and use your child's language where appropriate. Here are some examples of how you may do this:

'I can see you are upset.'

'That sounds hard.'

'That sounds scary. I get why that would be scary.'

'Tell me how that makes you feel.'

When children experience intense emotions, they often need someone to help them make sense of what is going on. By helping your child put their emotions and experiences into words, this can help them process the events and reduce the emotional intensity. Dr Tina Bryson and Dr Daniel Siegel coined the term *'name it to tame it'*, which encourages children to tell their 'stories' and name their emotions in order to help them to understand them better. We recommend reading their book *The Whole-Brain Child*. If your child struggles to talk when feeling intense emotions, they may first need to practise with a less verbal strategy, such as pointing at different 'feelings cards', to indicate which out of a range of emotions they are feeling at that moment. Then they can build up to telling you with actual words.

'A' Actions to soothe

We humans have an area in our brain called the pre-frontal cortex, which helps to regulate our impulses, drives and emotions. It is the part of our brain that helps us to make better choices and more rational responses. In contrast, our amygdala is the part of the brain that deals with threat. When we are in the threat system, our clever brain (pre-frontal cortex) shuts down. It switches off. This is why we may act in uncharacteristic ways when we are cross, scared or worried. The same is true for our children. In fact, their brains are much less developed than ours. There is evidence to suggest that our pre-frontal cortex does not develop fully until we are in our late twenties! So, they have a long way to go.

This is why, when our children are in the threat system, we need to help them return to a state where they can access their 'clever' brain. To do this, we need to activate their soothing system.

We know that when our children are in their threat system, this can often set off our own threat system. Unfortunately, this can mean that the parts of our brains that are talking to one another are neither logical, reasonable nor compassionate. In fact, when this occurs, it can often lead to an escalation between child and parent. Take the example of Mario:

Example

Mario is seven. He complained about his dinner because he felt he had been promised fish and chips, but was given spaghetti bolognese. Mario began moaning and refused to eat his dinner. His father had spent quite a bit of time cooking the meal and found he was getting more and more frustrated with Mario. In the example, we can see how this situation escalated:

Mario: I hate spaghetti. I'm not eating it.

Dad: I've spent ages making it. You're not having anything else.

Mario: Fine. I don't care.

Dad: You're so ungrateful!

Mario: I hate you! You never make me what I want!

Dad: Go to your room.

Mario: Nooo! *[screaming and shouting]*

Dad: I SAID GO TO YOUR ROOM! *[body language – moving towards Mario]*

Mario: *[screaming and shouting – hits out at Dad]*

As you can see from the example, when Mario's dad's threat system is triggered, the situation escalates. This highlights how important it is for parents to first engage in activities to calm and regulate themselves *before* we can begin to consider any parenting strategies.

1. Preparing yourself

As well as engaging your own soothing system, you will need to warm up and practise the 'version of yourself' that is going to be most helpful at implementing any of the following strategies with your child. This means thinking about what tone of voice you will use, your facial expression and how you will position yourself with your child.

Exercise 2: Tone matters

We would like you to say these two phrases in:

1.   a loud, monotonous way

2.   a soft, reassuring way

3.   a sarcastic tone

'That sounds incredibly hard'

'I understand'

Reflection: Ask yourself how you experienced these two sentences and which tone you would rather hear when being spoken to.

Your voice is affected by many things: pace, the intonation you use, the volume and your tone.

Exercise 3: Reading body language

Here are some pictures of different body positions and facial expressions. Take a moment to study each picture:

Think about which body language and facial expression you would you respond to better? Which body position and facial expression would your child respond to better?

It is built into us as humans to perceive some body language as more threatening and other postures and expressions as more receptive and safety seeking. We can replicate this effect in emojis and cartoons, too.

We would like you to practise using the tone of voice, facial expression and body posture you believe would be the wisest and most helpful with your child when they are struggling. Practise in the same way an actor might to get 'into role'. This may feel strange at first, but there is evidence suggesting that by 'acting' in a certain way (e.g. warm face, shoulders back and confident), this can actually lead us to *feel* that way. Isn't that incredible!

We both had this experience as trainee clinical psychologists. We were often in situations where we felt uncertain compared with our much more experienced colleagues. Both of us had to 'act' as the version we wanted to be (confident, reassuring, open). Over the months and years, we started to feel much more confident in our ability. An F1 racing driver doesn't win the Grand Prix on the first day. They have to practise, practise, practise. The same is true of practising body language and the version of us we would like to be when supporting our children.

Before you read on, we would like you to complete the following exercise:

Exercise 4: The version of yourself you would like to be with your child (body posture, facial expression and tone of voice)

Sit in an upright but comfortable position. Try to adopt a grounded, confident posture in your chair. Engage in your soothing breathing rhythm and friendly facial expression. Allow your breathing to slow a little and gently rest your attention on the flow of breathing in and breathing out. Stay with this for a minute or two.

Now, like an actor getting into role, you are going to use your imagination to create an outline of what you would be like as a deeply compassionate person. So, for a moment, think about the qualities you would have if this were the case. If it helps, take a moment to think about someone you know who is very compassionate. What are the qualities that make them a compassionate person? Remember, it doesn't matter whether you feel you are actually a compassionate person. The most important thing is to imagine that you have the qualities of a deeply compassionate person – you are stepping into this character, this version of you – just as actors do when they take on a role. Let's spend a minute imagining these qualities.

We are now going to focus on three specific qualities of compassion – wisdom, strength and caring commitment. We will focus on each in turn.

The first quality of your compassionate self is wisdom. There are many sources of wisdom: one comes from an understanding that we have tricky brains, which often get caught up in loops, or strong emotions and desires, that are difficult to manage. We didn't choose to have a mind that works like this. In fact, so much of who we are – our genes, our gender, our ethnicity or culture – we did not choose either, but this has had a significant impact on the person we are today. If we'd been raised by our next-door neighbours, rather than in our house by our caregivers, we would be a different person today. So your compassionate self has a deep wisdom about the nature of life itself, knows that so many of our problems are rooted in things that have been beyond our control – that much of what goes on in our minds is not our fault.

The wisdom of your compassionate self is also linked to learning how to take responsibility for doing something about your suffering. This involves stepping back from blame, shame and judgement and cultivating our minds in a way that might be helpful. Just as the grass, flowers and shrubs in a garden can grow in all sorts of ways, if we want it to look different we need to spend some time cultivating it. Our compassionate wisdom unfolds to help us learn and develop skills that help us alleviate the distress and difficulties we meet in life. Spend a minute or so focusing on what it would be like to be a wise person.

Now, bring to mind the quality of strength and authority. This strength emerges from both the wisdom of understanding the reality of distress and suffering in life, but also the commitment to do what we can about this. It involves courage to face difficulties and tolerate the discomfort they bring, as well as our fears about change. Imagine that your compassionate self is strong and has an inner confidence. Feel this connected to your upright body posture, feet grounded on the floor and breathing rhythm. Consider what tone of voice you would use, how you might stand and walk as a strong and confident person.

Finally, let's focus on the quality of commitment. Your compassionate self has a deep caring commitment. This is partly linked to an appreciation that life can be very hard and that we may all struggle with many things. So, given this, your compassionate self is motivated to be caring and is committed to alleviating your own and other people's suffering. It also has a desire to contribute to your own and other people's wellbeing, including your child's. It recognises that while many of our struggles are not our fault, we can take responsibility for acting in ways that are helpful and wise. Imagine how you would stand if you had a connection with this. Consider what your facial expression or your voice tone might be like if you were caring and committed to alleviating suffering. Spend a minute on this.

Now, let's apply this compassionate version of yourself to being with your child. Try to imagine these qualities – caring commitment, wisdom and strength – coming together into a sense of your compassionate self when you are with your child. Spend a minute or so imagining your compassionate self with these qualities. How might you stand? How might you speak when with your child? How might you think and feel when you are with them? How would you respond to them as your compassionate self? Focus on the desire to think, behave and feel compassionately. Don't worry if you do not feel that you have these qualities. Like an actor playing a character, just imagine what it would be like if you did.

Spend a couple of minutes allowing yourself to connect to your compassionate self when being with your child. Take your time on these different qualities. When you are ready, just let the image fade and note down any thoughts or insights following this exercise, including the version of yourself you want to be when addressing your child's struggles:

Notes:

Adapted with permission from *The Compassionate Mind Workbook* by Chris Irons and Elaine Beaumont

2.   De-escalation skills – How to manage threat system behaviours

When your child is firmly in their threat system, it is incredibly important to know what to do. Examples of behaviours that occur when a child is overwhelmed by this threat system are meltdowns, aggression, avoidance and panic attacks. These behaviours are often the ones that prompt families to seek support. Before moving into your compassionate parenting plan, it is important to upskill yourself to be able to manage your child's threat system.

Again, you will need to prepare and ensure that you are gearing up to this using all the skills discussed (body language, posture, tone of voice).

Remember, these skills will *not* reduce the likelihood of your child's struggles occurring, but they will help to reduce the severity of the behaviour in the moment.

Look at the table of dos and don'ts for supporting your child when they are engaging in threat system behaviours:

Dos	Don'ts
Stay calm, like a sat nav	Interrogate the person
Affirm and validate	Focus on punishment or consequences
Have one trusted person deal with the situation	Give comfort without permission
Confirm the feeling will go (feelings like waves)	Tell them to 'stay calm'
Reduce speech	Resort to emotional blackmail ('You make Mummy so sad')
Seek a safe place for solitude	Lose control

Sat nav example

A lovely example of implementing de-escalations skills is to pretend you are a sat nav. When we take a wrong turn, our critical mind often switches on to shout, 'You've gone the wrong way! You're going to be late! I can't believe you've done this!' The sat nav, however, calmly and confidently re-routes, letting you know the way. It does not offer judgement or appraisal, but calmly gives you another way to get to your destination. We would like you to aim to be like your child's sat nav during these times, calmly supporting them to get to their destination: to become regulated by accessing their soothing system.

3. Choosing your battles

There are often so many areas that we want to work on with our children. For example, their manners, saying sorry, learning to share, learning how to cope with big feelings, being polite, taking their dirty crockery back to the kitchen, and so on. This can make it difficult to let things go sometimes and parents may feel they are constantly raising problem areas with their kids. However, we know that this can lead to parental burnout and resentment from both parent and child. It is important to consider which battles are worth fighting for and which ones are OK to let go of. We recommend using a traffic-light system when considering the struggles your child may be having:

- The red priority concerns (these are the most important areas you want to work on)

- The amber areas (these are important but not essential)

- The green areas (these are the nice-to-haves, but are longer-term issues and it is not overly important to address them at the moment)

By thinking about which struggles fall into which area, parents can explore what they would like to work on first and give themselves permission to let other areas go for now.

Even with red priority concerns, it is important for us to learn when to push something and when to let things go. This links up with 'striking while the iron is cold', as we will see later.

4. Helping to increase your child's soothing system

We want you to consider what helps your child to feel safe and soothed. For some, this may be having a hug. For others, this may be retreating to a cosy space in their bedroom. Remember the diagram you drew of your child's three systems. It is important to help your child to increase their soothing strategies to get the right balance between each of the three systems.

It is incredibly important here to consider what makes *your child* feel soothed, as this may be different from what makes *you* feel better. Different emotions also warrant different responses.

Some children find physical contact more dysregulating when they are overwhelmed but may benefit from your physical presence in the room. Accounts from autistic children reveal that, for some, hugs can be aversive and illogical. Other children are really soothed by a cuddle and find this hugely beneficial.

Adolescence can often bring challenges when offering physical comfort due to the teenager's natural desire to move towards more independence. So it is important for you to consider your child's temperament, their age and stage, as well as their preferences. The safest way of offering physical comfort is to ask before giving. Let them know you are there for them no matter what they are feeling. This sets up a contract of trust with your child.

For some children, they need some space away from people to feel regulated. This could be a space in their bedroom or another area. This is not a punishment and needs to be set up before any escalation. Do this together when your child is calm. We will now think through some other ideas to help activate your child's soothing system.

Using your child's senses

When thinking about how to support your child to access their soothing system, we can often call upon the senses – sight, sound, touch and smell. Talk to your child about their senses and what helps them to feel good. Look at Worksheet 30 and tick any ways you believe you could help to shift your child's focus of attention using their senses:

Worksheet 30: Ways to shift your child's focus of attention using the senses

Sound	Touch	Sight	Smell	Taste
❑ Listening to music	❑ A gentle massage	❑ Looking at a picture of loved ones	❑ Essential oils	❑ Sucking on a mint
❑ Listening to the waves	❑ Massaging cream into your hands	❑ Imagining a safe place	❑ Perfume	❑ Having a cool drink
❑ Silence	❑ Cuddling	❑ Watching a film	❑ The smell of clean washing	❑ Chewing gum
❑ White noise	❑ Stroking (hair or skin)	❑ Drawing a picture		❑ Having a cup of herbal tea
❑ Classical music	❑ A cuddly blanket	❑ Colouring		❑ Having a snack
❑ Singing	❑ A bath			
	❑ Therapy putty			
	❑ Fidget toys			

Once you have an idea of the particular sense strategies that work for your child, we encourage you to support them in putting these into place. This may be by gently suggesting one of the strategies or having a 'soothing box' with the sensory strategies inside. This is discussed further in Chapter 6.

By supporting your child to focus on their senses in different ways, we are helping them to shift their focus of attention away from the threat and to be more present in the moment. It is also an activity that promotes mindfulness, a thread running throughout this book.

Breathing

When your child is in threat, we know that this can affect their body. If they were wearing a heart-rate monitor, it is likely that it would show an increased heart rate and shallower breathing. When our heart rate increases, we can feel light-headed, shaky and nauseous. We release cortisol and adrenaline when we are anxious, angry or stressed, which affects our body in many ways.

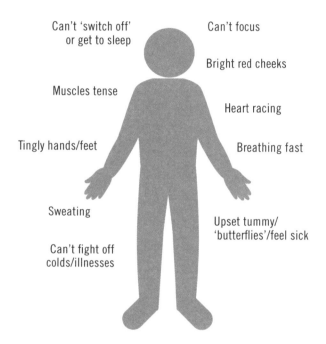

It can be really helpful to have a way of supporting children to slow their breathing down at times of stress, as this can help to engage their soothing system.

Neuroscientific evidence suggests that the most helpful breathing technique is 'rhythmic breathing', where you breathe in and out in time to a metronome. When we improve our ability to slow our heart rate down through simple breathing techniques, studies have shown that this can help decision-making, increase energy and reduce stress.

Everyone's rate of breathing is different. Our breathing rate tends to slow down as we get older, so it is important to work at your child's pace.

Here is an example of a breathing script for you to try with your child:

Breathing Script

Find a quiet place to sit. Sit in an upright position and gently bring a friendly expression to your face. Notice your breathing. Is it fast or slow? It is normal for our minds to wander off and think of other things. If you notice your mind is thinking about other things, try to gently bring it back to your breathing.

Imagine your belly is a balloon and when you breathe in you are blowing up the balloon. When you breathe out, you are letting all the air out of the balloon. You can put your hand on your tummy, just underneath your ribs to help with this.

As you are gently holding your attention to the flow of your breath, see if you can find a slower pace. Try to breathe in a smooth, even way, like a pendulum.

See if you can slow your breathing down a little bit. We can try counting to help with this. Try breathing in to the count of three. Once you've got to three, hold for one second before breathing out for three seconds. Like this:

Breathe in 1-2-3

Hold 1

Breathe out 1-2-3

Hold 1

Breathe in 1-2-3

Hold 1

Breathe out 1-2-3

Once you've practised this for a bit, you may want to try counting to four or five. Don't worry if this feels too slow. Just stay on three seconds as before. The more you practise, the slower your breathing will become.

Adapted with permission from *The Compassionate Mind Workbook* by Chris Irons and Elaine Beaumont

---

As with any new skill, it is important to practise this when your child is calm, rather than trying it for the first time when they are stressed or anxious. You may want to make it part of a bedtime or morning routine. Doing it as a whole family can help to instil these skills in daily life and let your child know that this is a skill that will benefit everyone. It may also be helpful to explain the science of rhythmic breathing to your child if they are reluctant to try it.

Muscle relaxation

Everyone is different and it is important to have different ways of supporting your child to calm. Some children really struggle with breathing techniques. If this is the case, then they may benefit from other ways of helping to calm the body. One such technique is progressive muscle relaxation. This is where you tighten one muscle group after another for around three seconds and then release, feeling the difference between relaxed muscles and tense muscles. This process can also help to ground the body and focus attention on different parts. As with breathing, it is important to practise this together with your child, when they are calm.

Relaxation script for children

Feet:

Pretend you are standing in a muddy puddle, with no shoes or socks on. Try to push your feet down into the bottom of the puddle. Feel your toes dig deep down into the squidgy mud. Spread your toes apart and push them deeper into the mud. Then relax your feet and toes. Let them go loose and floppy. Repeat.

Legs:

Pretend you have a balloon between your thighs. Imagine you are trying to pop the balloon by squeezing your thighs together. Keep squeezing that balloon. Now release the balloon and relax. Repeat.

Hands:

Pretend you are squeezing a whole orange in both your hands. Imagine you are trying to squeeze out all the juice. Feel the tightness in your hands as you squeeze. Now release the orange and see how your hands feel. Repeat.

Arms:

Now pretend you are squeezing an orange that is clamped in your armpit. Keep squeezing. Feel the tightness in your arms. Now release the orange and see how your arms feel. Repeat.

Shoulder:

Pull your shoulders up to your ears and push your head down into your shoulders. Hold this tight. Feel the tension in your shoulders. Now release and notice the difference. Do your shoulders feel lower or heavier? Repeat.

Jaw:

Imagine you have a giant gob-stopper in your mouth. It is very difficult to chew. Bite down on it hard! Now relax. Let your jaw go floppy. Notice the difference. Repeat.

Face:

Pretend there is an annoying fly that has landed on your cheek. You need to pretend to get the fly away without using your hands. Wrinkle and scrunch up your nose and forehead as much as you can. Now you can relax. Repeat.

Other children may benefit from 'heavy' tasks or deep pressure. Our occupational therapist colleagues often recommend such strategies for children based upon data from their proprioceptive system (the sense of self-movement, force and body position) and interoceptive system (the sense of our body's internal state). Items such as weighted blankets or deep pressure can restore a sense of calm to a child who feels overloaded and overwhelmed. But for other children, this would be dysregulating. Some children like to swing in a hammock or jump up and down on a trampoline, while others prefer stillness. So, again, be led by your child and ask for their opinion and consent. You may also wish to consult a qualified occupational therapist to ensure the strategy is the right fit for you child.

5.   Feelings like waves

Emotions can feel like thunder storms and tornadoes at times. But, like all weather systems, they move away with the passage of time. Sometimes this is what we need to do with our children – be with them while the storm passes.

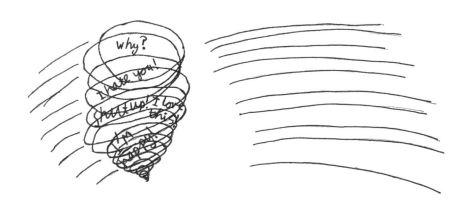

Once we have acknowledged how our child is feeling, it can be helpful to introduce the idea that the way they are feeling will not last for ever. We have worked to help many clients to see their feelings as transient, rather than fixed. One young person even had this motto tattooed on their body as a way of reminding them of this when times were hard.

Talking about your own experiences and emotions in a child-friendly way can help your child to acknowledge and normalise emotions and know that they will not last for ever. Take this example:

Example

Jane's daughter, Helen, came home in tears after a child at school had excluded her from a game and told her she was 'rubbish'. Jane comforted Helen with a cuddle and listened to her telling the story of what had happened. Jane asked curious questions and did not jump into 'teaching' mode. Helen told her mum about feeling sad and worried. Jane empathised with Helen and told her that it sounded like she'd had a tough day. Jane listened and, gradually, Helen's emotions started to ebb away. Jane was curious about Helen's experiences at school. This enabled Jane to gently introduce some coping and soothing methods.

When children experience powerful emotions (anxiety, shame, guilt, anger, sadness), narrative therapy suggests that it can be helpful to **externalise** the emotions. For example, by naming anxiety as 'worry bug'. By externalising the emotion, a young person can be empowered to make changes. This naming strategy often leads to creative and innovative discussions with children. Even for adolescents, this approach can be helpful.

Here are some ways we have helped children to effectively externalise problems:

Mr cloud   Worrymonster   Dr worry   Anger Gremlin

'S' Stopping with compassion

Within our S part, we are going to revisit the three core components of compassion:

1. Wisdom – to understand ourselves and our children

2. Strength – to face into difficult emotions and situations, rather than avoid them

3. Caring commitment – to alleviate distress in a way that is helpful and not harmful

Up until this point, we have not simply suggested strategies for parents to adopt. Rather we have asked you to understand your child's behaviour in the context of their genetics, temperament and experiences (the WISDOM part). We have then asked you to face into difficult emotions with your children, rather than avoid them (the STRENGTH part). Finally, we will consider how we can manage these difficult situations and find a way forward that will be helpful for you and your child (CARING COMMITMENT).

With so many parenting strategies out there, the big question is how do you pick and apply the right one to use that will be most helpful to your child and family?

In this section, we will consider ways of applying parenting approaches wisely, flexibly and COMPASSIONATELY. These strategies are an integration of well-researched parenting and therapeutic approaches, such as positive discipline (Jane Nelsen), the whole-brain child (Dr Daniel Siegel, Dr Tina Bryson), narrative therapy, acceptance and commitment therapy and cognitive behavioural therapy. However, at the heart of the strategies we have chosen is compassion.

When any of these approaches are applied without compassion, it can be perceived as punitive and can compromise parent–child relationships. These approaches require flexibility and patience. They require collaboration with your child and for them to be an active participant in the process. They aim to support your child to find ways to overcome struggles, to build their own confidence and lifelong skills.

Remember, every struggle is different. Here are some key suggestions for you to consider when parenting your child and the struggles they may be

encountering. We urge you to use compassion as the groundwork for implementing any plan.

1. Alignment

Parents often have differing views on how to manage their children's struggles. For example, one parent will be more lenient while the other is just a little too strict. Or one parent tends to be very lenient until pushed too far, when they will oscillate to super-strict. This difference is apparent in parents or carers who are together or separated, with step-parents, and for single parents when there are significant others involved (e.g. a grandparent or new partner). We have witnessed so many examples of this in our clinical work. What can happen is a tug of war, where each parent becomes more embedded in their approach, pulling further backward from the other. Unfortunately, there have even been times where this struggle has contributed to parental separation.

Unfortunately, wisdom (research and experience) tells us that misaligned parents/carers, no matter what their stance, are less effective than parents who are aligned.

With our compassionate stance, we need to consider how to become more aligned, but this is not always easy. Hopefully, the process of going through this book helps with that. It may be useful to read this book with your partner and explore a plan that everyone can stick to. Family meetings can be a helpful way of doing this as everyone gets a say and the family members come up with a solution together. The second chapter focuses on your own experience of being parented and this might be worth coming back to for both you and the other parent/carer. Remember, becoming more aligned can take effort and needs revising regularly.

2.   Fundamentals for your child

We would like you to ask yourself some key questions:

- Is my child getting enough sleep?

- Is my child getting enough downtime/soothing time?

- Is my child eating a balanced diet?

- Is my child drinking enough fluid?

- Is my child getting enough exercise?

If the answer is no to any of these questions, then this may be having a negative impact on their behaviour. We know that lack of sleep can make us much less able to tolerate emotions. We all have experience of this over the years of parenting! Not enough sleep can also make it harder for us to learn and think in our normal way. It puts us at greater risk of mental health issues, too.

Along with a lack of sleep, there is research that shows us that what we eat affects how we feel and behave. For example, Dr Ben Feingold has claimed that certain children have an intolerance to salicylates, which are found in many natural foods. Other children have an intolerance to the E numbers that are added to a great many processed foods – and often the foods marketed specifically for children. Feingold claims that eliminating these types of foods from these children's diets would radically change their behaviour. We live in a world of processed foods filled with sugar and other preservatives. We know that food has a direct effect on health and wellbeing. Sometimes making small changes can make a large difference.

Another very important consideration is the environment your child is in. Sometimes, it is the environment that needs to change and not your child. Every child is different, just like every adult is different. For us adults, we often get to choose where we work and where we live, or at least we have some control over this sort of decision. Children have very little choice.

Unfortunately, our schooling system also provides little choice and variety. Specialist settings or innovative schools doing things differently are few and far between or require funding to get a place. Nonetheless, we have supported many young people to move schools and this has had an enormous impact on their mental wellbeing.

Example

Take Muhammed. He was two years old when he began nursery. Initially, he started off in a quiet, tiny room with a few very caring, older carers. After a few weeks, he moved to another room, where there were more children and a much higher ratio of boys to girls. Muhammed began to become incredibly distressed at home and was having frequent meltdowns. He also began showing intense separation anxiety when dropped off at the nursery. Luckily, his mother spotted that Muhammed was very unhappy in this setting and found him a different environment, one that was quieter with fewer children. Muhammed moved to a Montessori Village pre-school. Almost immediately, his behaviour improved and he showed less anxiety at being separated from his mother.

We can see from this example what a marked effect this setting had on Muhammed. This does not mean that we simply need to change schools or childcare settings at the first sign of an issue. But it is important to consider whether the environment is right for your child.

3.   Fundamentals for your family: getting closer and carving out quality time

In a busy family, it is often easy to overlook how important spontaneous acts of generosity, compassion and kindness towards your child can be. It can be incredibly powerful to reinforce just how important they are to you and how much you value them before problems arise. This can be achieved by means of simple strategies, such as spontaneously buying them a t-shirt because you thought they would like it or by playing their favourite song in the car on the way to school because you know they are tired and would prefer to listen rather than chat. Carving out time together is also important, as we will explore later.

In some families, their struggles have significantly reduced the positive time parents spend with their child. However, it is well documented in many parenting approaches that spending quality time with our children is incredibly important. This is time when there are no demands and we can just 'be' with our children. It is important for this time to be child-led and should help to enhance our connection with them.

Carving out this time does not mean spending lots of money or re-arranging work. It is about being creative with the time you have. Take this example:

Example

For the Caravaggio family, their special time was a movie night and a homemade curry every Friday. They also made sure they had a roast every other Sunday lunch together. These events were integrated into the daily routine of their week and the children looked forward to them. The children's parents had to ensure that they said no to any invites that clashed with this time or discussed it as a family before agreeing to a change. The children also decided to have some 1:1 time with each parent every month, where they went to get a drink together at the local café.

Here are some ideas for carving out time:

- Movie night

- Letting your child show you their favourite memes

- Playing your child on a computer game, or watching them while they game

- Playing a board game

- Having a food theme night (everyone helps make a dish)

- Going to the park

- Playing football in the garden

- Hide and seek

- Spending time hearing about special interests

- Playing make believe

- Creating a 'show'

- Going for a walk with your child

Take five minutes to think about ways you can try to get closer to your child and carve out time with them. Jot them down in Worksheet 31:

Worksheet 31: Ways for you to get closer and carve out time with your child

4. Fundamentals for your family: compassionate household boundaries

It can be very helpful to establish clear boundaries within families, boundaries that are drawn up either together as a family or collaboratively as parents. These boundaries help our children know what your expectations are of them and also what their expectations should be of you. This can sometimes eliminate the need for further parenting strategies.

Here is an example of household boundaries written together during a family meeting between Grayson, his sister and their parents. Each person had a say and they came up with ideas that were written up and put on the fridge.

Household boundaries

1.   *Help each other out*

2.   *Treat each other the way we want to be treated*

3.   *Take responsibility for our things*

4.   *Try to make it better if we make a mistake*

5.   *Respect everyone's body rules*

6.   *Give people courage when they're crying*

7.   *Care for each other*

8.   *Listen to people's ideas*

Once you have an outline of the household rules, it can be especially helpful to agree to them as a family. This lays the foundations for skill building, problem-solving and what happens when we or our children do not stick to these boundaries.

When thinking about your household boundaries, it can be helpful to outline one of the core components of compassion: that anything suggested needs to be <u>helpful and not harmful to the self and others</u>. This can be a benchmark for the discussion.

Having regular family meetings can help the family explore these boundaries together, to modify them, if necessary, and opens pathways to solving problems.

5.   Redefining your child's difficulties

Many parenting strategies focus on what not to do, rather than exploring how to overcome or solve a problem. Therefore, we would like you to 'flip' the focus of the difficulties your child is experiencing to focus instead on what your child needs to work on. See this example:

Example

Struggles	FLIP	To work on
Hitting and kicking		Managing big emotions
Meltdowns		Increasing soothing time
		Learning how to cope with coming off games
Fear of spiders		Building on bravery and learning spiders are OK
Getting along with friends		Learning how to take turns with ideas
		Learning how to calmly tell people how I feel
Leaving all the washing on the floor		Helping each other more with house tasks

In Worksheet 32 we would like you to compassionately consider your child's struggles (noted down in the previous chapter on page 74) and then FLIP them around to areas to be worked on collaboratively.

Worksheet 32:

Struggles	FLIP	To work on

6.   Striking while the iron is cold

As discussed in earlier chapters, when we are in our threat system, it is incredibly hard, if not impossible, to think rationally and logically.

When trying to implement ANY plan or strategy to support your child with their behaviour, it is therefore incredibly important to strike when the iron is cold. This means taking time and space with your child to explore their struggles in more detail. Implementing any of the following ideas while a child is in a heightened state of emotion is likely to result in your child rejecting these ideas, leading to further struggle. For children who experience difficulties when talking about these subjects, the plan may need to be addressed over multiple occasions and with the support of another person. If there is a sign that your child is becoming distressed, then you will need to stop and come back to it at a later time.

Tips for keeping the iron cold:

- Choose a setting that is calming for your child
- Consider talking to them 'side on' (in the car or while on a walk). This means you are both facing forward, which naturally makes the conversation less threatening
- For teenagers, you may want to message (WhatsApp, text) them to start the conversation
- Keep the conversation light and collaborative
- Don't talk for too long. Say you can talk again soon
- Sometimes some light collaborative humour can help. This is laughing *with* but not *at*. For other children, humour should be avoided

7.   Collaborative compassionate solutions

When beginning to explore specific parenting approaches to support your child with any struggles, we want to foster and develop a *collaborative approach*, that puts them at the centre of the process. Take a look at Exercise 5:

Exercise 5: Idea generator

We would like you to think of a time when you have had an idea or plan thrust upon you without time to think about it and without being consulted. This may have been at work, or from your family or friends. Note down how you felt about this:

Now we would like you to think of a time when you were involved in developing a new idea or change – time when your ideas were listened to and considered. This could be at work or at home. Note down how you felt about the process. Did it make a difference that you were consulted and your ideas were respected?

This example highlights how we often feel much more positive about making changes when we are prepared, included and considered. The same is true of our children.

We need to think about how to approach these conversations with our children. Children can shut down when they are faced with a discussion about the issues they are having. Their critical mind will be a powerful factor within this. Shame is an emotion that leads us all to shut down and can be a powerful inhibitor to change, too. Take a look at Exercise 6:

Exercise 6: How shame feels

Consider a time when you have done or said something that made you feel ashamed. Spend a moment thinking about this time. Focus on how you feel in your body. What do you notice? What is running through your mind? What does this feeling make you want to do or not do?

Note down any thoughts:

Take a moment to focus on your soothing breathing rhythm before coming back to this book.

We know that shame can be a powerful emotion that can make us shut down and clam up. It can make us want to deny or protest, to make excuses. Therefore, in order to try to support our child with their struggles, we want to stay away from methods that make them feel shame, even if this is not our intention. Unfortunately many well-meaning strategies (e.g. 'naughty step', 'sun and the sad side' chart) have left children feeling a sense of shame and reinforce aspects of their critical mind. They may provide a short-term solution, but the longer-term impact can be unhelpful.

A key aspect of collaborative solutions is drawing upon your child's ability to find their own solutions to their struggles. This may be explored in a one-to-one discussion with your child or it may be more appropriate to tackle as a family, within a family meeting. As psychologists, we often have discussions with children about solutions and it always amazes us how creative and innovative children are.

Example

Izzy is ten years old and came to our clinic with her parents. She spoke about feeling very worried about going on holiday, including getting to the holiday destination and being away from home. Initially, Izzy was withdrawn and shy in sessions. She found it hard to listen to the conversation as her parents were telling us about how she would cry, scream, ruminate and struggle to sleep. Izzy worked with her psychologist to learn about anxiety and how it is a normal human emotion. She was then asked to come up with solutions. Izzy was incredible. She spent the session talking about ways she and her parents could work together to overcome her struggles. This excerpt is from Izzy:

'Mission Is Now Possible' Plan:

- Remember what I know about anxiety

- Plan for the week before you fly: go to the shops to create a distraction box, do some exercise and get enough sleep. This will help with anxiety

- Remember holidays that have been fun in the past

- Distractions at the airport, such as soft play or shopping

- Use my meditation app

- Remember to eat, otherwise I will feel sick and dizzy

- Lots of hugs from my mum and dad

- Know the facts! Anxiety feels bad but doesn't mean I am in danger. I can cope and have done it before

- Focus on the real stuff, don't spend time on the 'what ifs'

- Get lost in a book ☺

This example involved Izzy having a discussion just with her parents. However, sometimes it can be helpful to discuss and solve problems at a family meeting, where the whole family takes responsibility to generate solutions and stick to these.

Example

Jane and John had three kids, Luke (ten), Matty (eight) and Sienna (four). Before bedtime, the children would have showers and would often leave their clothes strewn over the floor. During one family meeting, Jane and John raised this. They acknowledged that this was their problem and asked the children to help them find a solution. The children quickly came up with the idea that clothes left on the floor and not in the washing basket would be put in a box and left unwashed until they were eventually put in the washing basket. They agreed that Sienna may need a bit more help with this as she was younger and Luke and Matty both agreed to remind and support her. On one occasion, Matty left his dirty school PE kit on the floor, which was put in the box by Mum. The next week, on the day Matty needed his PE kit, he realised it was dirty. As Matty had helped to come up with the solution, he was not surprised to see that the kit had not been washed. Matty had to wear a different shirt and shorts to school that day. This was the last time he left his PE kit on the floor.

---

8.   Reward systems

Sometimes your child may need extra motivation in the early days to follow the newly designed compassionate strategy. We know how hard it is to change our own habits at first and the same is true for our children. Therefore, rewards can help focus their mind.

However, reward systems are not designed to be long-term solutions. We have many parents come to us, saying that the reward system has only 'worked' for a short period of time. This is normal. I am sure you can identify with getting bored or becoming forgetful about using a reward system after several weeks and your child can become bored with them, too. Therefore, the best reward systems need to be creative and updated regularly.

Here are two examples of reward systems in action:

Example 1

Elsie is seven years old. She has been struggling with separation anxiety from her mother and finds attending clubs and playdates very hard. Elsie learnt about the role of anxiety and how this makes us believe something is frightening and dangerous when it is actually safe. Elsie and her mother explored ways to make her feel more comfortable with playdates and clubs and gradually face her fears. They wrote down a number of steps Elsie could take in graded order (e.g. 1st step: going to best friend's house and Mum leaving for five minutes. 2nd step: going to ballet and Mum sitting outside the door, etc.). Then they devised a jigsaw reward system. This involved printing out a picture of a special reward (a doll) and then cutting it into jigsaw pieces. Each time Elsie took a step towards facing her fears, she gained a piece of the jigsaw puzzle. Once she had all the pieces, Elsie got her doll. This system enabled Elsie to keep going with facing her fears, gradually working towards attending her clubs and playdates without her mum. She was able to learn that her mum would return and that everything would be OK.

Example 2

Thomas is a thirteen-year-old boy who struggles to regulate his emotions around his younger sister, Maddie. He frequently shouts at her, calling her names and goading her into arguments. The family sat down together and discussed how they would like the household to be calmer. Each person discussed how they could make things easier for the other. For Thomas, the goal was for him to take himself away to his bedroom when Maddie annoyed him and then tell his parents what she had done to 'wind him up', so they could address it later. They agreed that if he could work on this, then he could earn some money to spend how he wishes (e.g. online game or going out with friends).

Thomas initially found it hard to take himself to his room, but he was motivated to earn some money for a cinema trip coming up and so tried hard to take himself away when Maddie annoyed him. His parents were able to speak with Maddie about respecting Thomas's wishes, which made Thomas feel heard. The whole family were able to reflect upon how things were happier and calmer in the household. Thomas earned his money for his cinema trip. This reward gave him an initial prompt to do things differently, but Thomas also gained some internal motivation to continue this strategy as he learnt it would actually benefit him in the future (e.g. by feeling heard by his parents and less upset and cross).

9.   Logical consequences

This section is at the bottom of the parenting tool kit, although for many parents and professionals, this will be the first place they start.

Many parenting approaches discuss the use of consequences for behaviour. Unfortunately, consequences are often misinterpreted and misused and become *punishment*. Punishments can appear to show results in the short term for parents (e.g. getting the child to do what they want) but in the longer term the effect on your relationship will be negative and could lead to resentment, rebellion and retreat. Jane Nelsen talks about this concept in her books on positive discipline and how the strategy of 'logical consequences' is often misused by parents and teachers, creating negative effects.

A very clear example of the use of misguided behaviour management strategies is the 'sun and the cloud' or 'smiley and sad face' system, often used in classrooms. The sad face or cloud may lead to the consequence of loss of play. We have seen how the use of such methods can leave children feeling dejected, shamed and demotivated, particularly as it highlights the child's undesirable behaviour for all the class to see. It can also feel confusing, because a child may not be pre-warned about the consequences of their behaviour. In addition, because the consequence does not directly relate to the child's problematic behaviour, it can end up feeling like a punishment. For example, if a child had completed their classwork and then started throwing paper balls around the classroom . . .

An unhelpful consequence = loss of playtime

A logical consequence = the child picking up all the paper balls they have thrown

Jane Nelsen notes that there can be times when logical consequences are helpful, but they need to be age appropriate, helpful and used in an appropriate way. They also need to be respectful and encouraging to children, helping them to learn responsibility and accountability. She talks about the four Rs of logical consequences. These should be:

1. *Related*

2. *Respectful*

3. *Reasonable*

4. *Revealed in advance*

If the logical consequence is a loss of privilege, then it can be helpful to talk to your child about the concept of responsibility and privilege. Humans (adults and children) have fundamental basic human rights. The right to have food, shelter, water, love and care. The right to be respected, treated equally and be born free from harm and neglect. Privilege is different. Privileges may be toys, gaming, sweets and screens. With privilege comes responsibility. The responsibility to look after the privileges and the responsibility to behave in a way that is not harmful to you or others.

Responsibility = privilege

Lack of responsibility = loss of privilege

It can be helpful to talk to children about this in more detail. Talk about what a privilege is and their responsibility for keeping these privileges. This helps us to stick to the four Rs of logical consequence. For example, as adults, we need to earn money to buy ourselves both essential and luxury items. When we buy luxury items, if we do not look after them, they can break. When they break, that is it, unless we earn more money to pay for another item. Either way, we experience a logical consequence. We meet with many children and adolescents who have become fixated on gaming and see it as a basic right, rather than a privilege. This can result in it becoming unhelpful to them and to those around them. Take the example of Jack:

Example

Jack is ten years old and was having regular aggressive meltdowns where he would hit, punch and throw objects at his parents when they asked him to stop playing Fortnite. *His parents felt paralysed by the situation, as he would repetitively ask and plead for games when not gaming and then, when he started, would have a tantrum when he was asked to stop. Jack and his parents worked with their psychologist to begin to see gaming as a privilege – one that came with responsibility. The responsibility to stop playing when asked, and to only game at certain times due to the impact upon his health and wellbeing and his responsibility to do other tasks first (homework).*

Jack and his parents worked together to find solutions to this problem and agree what would happen if there was a lack of responsibility. This was done with an underlying premise of compassion and his parents reiterated to Jack that they loved him very much and wanted to work together to support him. They all agreed that Jack would have a fifteen-minute warning and then it was his responsibility to stop playing. If he was not able to do this, then Jack was not yet ready for the responsibility of playing games and the logical consequence was that his Xbox would be put away. They agreed that this would be done the day after, when 'the iron was cold', and that he would need to build up to playing Fortnite *in the future, by practising with less addictive games or building other areas of interest.*

Here we can see how Jack is involved with the decision-making around the solution. Jack was prepared for the new system and knew what would happen next if he struggled to stop playing his games. They had also agreed on time scales and framed this in a way that made Jack feel in control of the outcome.

10.   Natural consequences

By contrast, a natural consequence is something that happens naturally. It occurs with no adult interference. For example, if your child goes out to play in the rain without a coat on, the natural consequence is that they will get wet and cold. Natural consequences can be an ideal opportunity for children to learn. However, as parents, we often tend to step in and 'rescue' our children from them. For example, how many times have you sat with your child cajoling them to do their homework, packed their bags for them or demanded they wear their coat outside? It is understandable that we should want to alleviate distress for our children, but it is important to ask ourselves whether this is supportive for our children in the longer term. If the answer is no, then this is an area we may need to begin to work on. Of course, there are times when natural consequences are certainly *not* appropriate. These include:

- When the natural consequence puts your child or others in danger (e.g. leaning out of a second-floor window, playing near a busy road)

- If your child is not yet developmentally ready for the expectations that have been set (e.g. we would not expect a child younger than six to show awareness of road safety)

- When your child's threat system is already firing too strongly

- When the outcome of your child's behaviour is not a problem to them (e.g. if they eat junk food for every meal, do not wash, brush their teeth or do their homework)

Bringing it all together with compassion

We would now like you to put together a compassionate parenting plan to support your child with their struggles. This includes your intentions to support them to alleviate distress, the strategies you feel would be most useful and how to apply these with compassion. Here is an example of how to bring a parenting plan together:

Example

Ted and Sally are parents to Mia (six years old). They created the following plan to help cope with Mia's intense meltdowns. Both parents considered how they could apply the parenting strategies compassionately, based upon their work from the previous chapters.

Strategy	How to apply with compassion
Preparing myself for Mia's meltdowns	*Practise the calm, caring version of myself by using breathing and imagery. Do this when I wake up in the morning each day for a few minutes*
	Find a place to take myself to if I start getting cross
	Be compassionate to myself by saying, 'Iron cold, I am only human'
Agree a collaborative strategy with everyone	*Set up a family meeting together where we can talk about our household boundaries and how we manage these*
	Family meetings to be held in the morning, as Mia is fresher and can concentrate better
Helping Mia to get back into the soothing system	*Creating a soothing space for Mia*
	Talk to Mia about things that make her feel better
	Practise these strategies with her before bedtime
	Ask for permission before giving Mia a hug when she is having a meltdown
	Understand that it may not always be easy for Mia to control her emotions. She is only six
Naming the emotions	*Find a time to talk about this. Talk about my own feelings and how I can feel cross sometimes, too*
Create special time	*Consider what Mia's interests are and enlist her support in carving out time for this. Ensure it works for us both and I can put away my mobile during this time, as it can take me away from the moment. Talk to other parent about when this works for them*

Before you start to build your own compassionate parenting plan, we would like you to re-engage with those three core components of compassion: wisdom, strength and caring commitment. Take a moment to engage in the following exercise:

Exercise 7: Compassionate parenting plan exercise

Sit in an upright but comfortable position. Try to adopt a grounded, confident posture in your chair. Engage in your soothing breathing rhythm and friendly facial expression. Allow your breathing to slow a little and gently rest your attention on the flow of breathing in and breathing out. Stay with this for a minute or two.

Now, like an actor getting into role, you are going to use your imagination to create an outline of what you would be like as a deeply compassionate person. Remember, it doesn't matter whether you feel you are actually a compassionate person. The most important thing is to imagine that you have the qualities of a deeply compassionate person – you are stepping into this character, this version of you – just as actors do when they take on a role. Let's spend a minute imagining these qualities.

We are now going to focus on three qualities of compassion – wisdom, strength and caring commitment. We will focus on each in turn.

The first quality of your compassionate self is wisdom. There are many sources of wisdom: one comes from an understanding that we have tricky brains, which often get caught up in loops, or strong emotions and desires, that are difficult to manage. We didn't choose to have a mind that works like this. In fact, so much of who we are – our genes, our gender, our ethnicity or culture – we did not choose either, but this has had a significant impact on the person we are today. If we'd been raised by our next-door neighbours, rather than in our house by our caregivers, we would be a different person today. So your compassionate self has a deep wisdom about the nature of life itself, knows that so many of our problems are rooted in things that have been beyond our control – that much of what goes on in our minds is not our fault.

The wisdom of your compassionate self is also linked to learning how to take responsibility for doing something about your child's suffering. This involves stepping back from blame, shame and judgement and cultivating our minds in a way that might be helpful to your child. Our compassionate wisdom unfolds to help us learn and develop skills that help us alleviate the distress and difficulties our child may be going through. Spend a minute or so focusing on what it would be like to be a wise person.

Now, bring to mind the quality of strength and authority. This strength emerges from both the wisdom of understanding the reality of distress and suffering in life, but also the commitment to do what we can about this. It involved courage to face into your child's difficulties and tolerate the discomfort they bring, as well as our fears about change. Imagine that your compassionate self is strong and has an inner confidence; feel this connected to your upright body posture, feet grounded on the floor and breathing rhythm.

Finally, let's focus on the quality of commitment. Your compassionate self has a deep caring commitment – this is partly linked to an appreciation that life can be very hard, and that we may all struggle with many things and so, too, with our children. So, given this, your compassionate self is motivated to be caring and committed to alleviate your own and your child's suffering. It also has a desire to contribute to your own and other people's wellbeing, including your child's. It recognises that while many of our struggles are not our fault, we can take responsibility for acting in ways that are helpful and wise for us and our child. Imagine how you would stand if you had a connection with this. Consider what your facial expression or your voice tone might be like if you were caring and committed to alleviating suffering. Spend a minute on this.

Now, let's apply this compassionate version of yourself when thinking about the struggles your child is going through. How may this version of yourself act in the face of these struggles? Drawing upon your wisdom, what would be the most helpful way forward? Connect with how this version of yourself may apply these strategies. How would you hold yourself when around your child? What would your tone of voice be like? How would you convey this deep commitment to support your child?

Spend a couple of minutes allowing yourself to connect to your compassionate self and how they may formulate a plan to support your child. Take your time on these different qualities. When you are ready, just let the image fade and then go to Worksheet 33.

Now write down any strategies you would like to explore with your child and consider how you can apply these compassionately, to yourself, to your child and to other people:

Worksheet 33: Compassionate parenting strategies suitable for your child

Strategy	How will you apply this compassionately?

Getting it wrong

Despite our best efforts, it is completely normal to get parenting wrong sometimes. It can be particularly hard when we are overtired, overworked and stressed about other parts of our life. Or when our child is really struggling with either their emotions or their behaviour, or both. There can also be particular issues that trigger us that do not trigger other parents. For example, one parent we worked with could not stand whinging and whining, whereas another parent coped well with this but found the idea of their child being sad unbearable.

There will be times when, despite your best efforts and motivation, you end up parenting in a way you didn't plan to. This is normal. Even the most compassionate parent will have these times, because we are all human.

If this happens, the first thing to remember is not to panic. Occasionally, getting it wrong can, in fact, model to your child that nobody is perfect. What you do next is then incredibly important. Your focus would now be on repair and re-stabilising the connection with your child, using warmth.

Before you act, you may need to go through EASE again, to spot what you are feeling and to introduce an action to soothe, so that you are then in the best place possible to deal with the next step of repair and reconnection. You may also need to plan what parenting strategy is the wiser and more helpful approach. Before you speak to your child, you may need to help them with a soothing strategy.

It takes a lot of courage to say 'I got this wrong' to your child. But our wisdom tells us that this is key for moving forward in your journey as a compassionate parent to your child. You can then deal with the situation that has just happened in the way you had planned out. It is never too late to take a compassionate approach.

'E' Emotions now?

The last part of the EASE strategy is to reflect on what you've just done and the impact of your compassionate mind parenting strategies on your child's feelings, their mind and their behaviours.

We often find that our compassionate mind can ease the difficult emotions in others and ourselves and help us to consider more helpful ways of moving forward for our child and ourselves.

Look back to your hopes and wishes for your child at the beginning of Chapter 4 and, after connecting with your compassionate mind, consider these again. Which approach seems more helpful to you: approaching these hopes and fears with the critical or the compassionate mind?

Challenges

Many parents have experienced the following statements, either from their own critical mind, or from others:

They're just naughty

You are too soft

It is bad parenting that causes this behaviour

That wouldn't have happened under my roof

You're too hard

You're not cut out for this

You should do it like this

Whether they are from our own mind or from the perspectives of others, they can wobble us and steer us off track. If you have worked through a plan and it is beneficial for you and your child, then it is OK not to listen to these challenges and instead to use your strength, wisdom and caring commitment to continue with your plan.

We understand that the pathway to parenting compassionately can be tricky. But we urge you to stick with it and to bring your mind back to the work you have completed so far. Re-reading the chapters and setting aside time to practise some of the exercises can help. It may be helpful to connect with people who share your views or to encourage those who are critical to read this book.

Remember, life can be hard; parenting is hard. By reading this book and spending this time considering your own parenting style and the needs of your child, you are already on the pathway to compassionate parenting. Keep going!

In summary

It is helpful to hold in mind the EASE strategy with your child. This includes:

- Acknowledging the range of your child's emotions, and the impact these emotions have on their body, their mind and their actions

- Preparing yourself to support your child

- Supporting your child with strategies to soothe their threat system, such as: using your child's senses, breathing exercises, muscular relaxation and the idea of feelings being like waves

- Creating a compassionate parenting plan, which incorporates alignment between parents; ensuring your child's sleep, rest and diet are in the right balance; carving out quality time; developing compassionate household boundaries; re-defining your child's difficulties; striking while the iron is cold; collaboratively generating solutions; using reward systems as appropriate; and applying logical and natural consequences

6 Developing a Compassionate Mind in Your Child

As parents, we often have to deal with multiple tricky situations with our children. However, one of the hardest emotionally is when we hear our child being really critical towards themselves and we know that, in that moment, they mean it.

Such comments pull on our heartstrings and our natural instinct is to respond quickly with a statement denying it, such as saying, 'No you're not,' or trying to correct it, such as responding with, 'Don't say that; of course you're clever.'

These responses are hard to resist, as we're keen to take away our children's upset and critical mind, to try to make them feel better. However, there is a danger that by shutting down such comments so quickly, we are risking:

1.   Our children feeling we don't truly listen

2.   Our children feeling we can't 'handle' the truth about them

3.   Our children feeling invalidated

So what can we do instead?

Our goal is to help our children develop the courage and determination to address this critical part of their mind, through building their own compassionate mind. As Paul Gilbert describes, this compassionate mind can then allow our children to nurture, look after, teach, guide, mentor, soothe, protect and offer feelings of acceptance and belonging to themselves.

The first step is to help our children understand their own emotional systems. We can then support them to recognise if these systems are balanced and what to do if things aren't feeling quite right.

Teaching our children about the emotional regulation systems

To help our children become experts in detecting whether they are in a soothing, drive or threat system, we initially need to share with them Paul Gilbert's model of the three emotional regulation systems. Dr Mary Welford, a consultant clinical psychologist who is an expert in compassion-focused therapy for younger people, suggests making this three systems model 'child friendly' and using language that makes sense to them.

Colour coding the three systems model

In our clinic, we find it helpful to use a different colour for each emotional regulation system, as this helps children to remember which system they are in. The colours that tend to be used are:

Green – for the soothing system

Blue – for the drive system

Red – for the threat system

Thus, children can often refer to the 'colour they are in' rather than the name of the system; this is easier for them. For example, saying, 'Mum, I'm feeling red right now.' You can even support your child to write out their own version of the three-system model using their own unique colour code and maybe using different coloured pens for each system. For example:

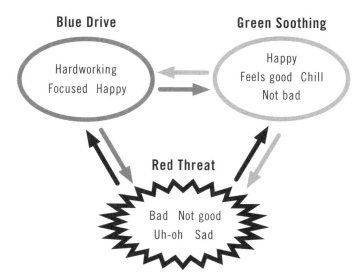

If your child likes the colour coding system, there are several ways to explore this model using the three colours, including:

Draw on a big piece of paper the three systems and chat about what each one feels like for your child	Have a blue, a green and a red cushion. Take it in turns for your child to sit on each cushion and tell you about each one of their systems
Put red, green and blue pieces of paper on the floor, and walk across them, discussing each system	Take each colour in turn and cook with food from each colour, discussing each system. For example: **Green:** green apples, celery, cucumber, lettuce, green jelly babies and other green sweets **Red:** red apples, tomatoes, strawberries, cherries, red Skittles and other red sweets **Blue:** blueberries, blackberries, blue cheese, blue Smarties and other blue sweets
Take it in turns to throw red, blue and green bean bags into a pot, or emptied waste paper bin. Discuss what each of the colours means as your child throws the bean bags	Make three posters with your child about each system; using green, red or blue pens to write on each of the corresponding posters

Undertake an art project, using the three colours to explore the three systems	Blow up red, green and blue balloons to discuss the model with them. You could even write on to the balloons with a permanent marker, to record what each system is like for your child
Make jewellery with blue, red and green beads, while discussing each system	Kick red, blue and green balls into a goal in turn. Chat about each of the systems as you kick in the ball of the corresponding colour

Spend a few minutes thinking about your child's preferred way of learning. Would they like the colour coding system? If so, which of the above ideas work best to teach your child about the three emotional regulation systems? Jot down a plan in Worksheet 34:

Worksheet 34: My ideas for teaching my child about the three emotional regulation systems:

(How are you going to do this? When is the best time to do it?)

As we all know, in order to learn a new skill, we generally have to keep practising it over and over again, until we get better at it – whether that is cooking, a sporting activity or even DIY. Learning about the three emotional regulation systems and our emotions is the same. After introducing them to your child, you need to support them to practise working out which system they are in; until they are an expert in this skill.

If you have an older child, it might be that you can help them practise spotting their different systems by:

- Having a daily conversation about the three systems they've spotted being in over the course of the day

- Asking your child to keep a diary for the day and then challenge them to spot which systems they were in for each diary entry. They can use the red, blue and green colour scheme for their diary entries if they find it useful

Younger children may be able to practise by:

- Being in a soothing system with you, such as both of you listening to calming music and letting your child notice how their body feels when relaxed. You could also do this with the drive system; for example, setting them a challenge they would enjoy (e.g. helping you build a tower of blocks as quickly as possible), and discussing how their body feels as they undertake the challenge

- Communicating which system they're in using a colour scheme. For example, putting on the correct coloured hat or jewellery to represent their emotional regulation system, having a key ring with small cards with each of the colours on them, and showing this to you when prompted, or sitting on the correctly coloured cushion to communicate their emotional regulation system in a given moment

You can continue to develop your children's understanding of the three systems by chatting to them about which one of the different systems you (as a parent) are in within a given moment. For example:

'This queue for the post office is sooo long. I can feel myself going into a threat system and I am feeling quite stressed.'

'I'm feeling completely soothed right now, watching *Gym Stars* on TV with you.'

'Right, I'm getting into a full drive system, so I've got the energy to cook our dinner!'

The right balance?

Once your child is skilled at spotting their different emotional regulation systems, you can chat to them about whether or not the balance of these three states is right for them.

For example, if your child is getting stressed about a piece of homework, you might chat about how they are working so hard in their drive system that you think it might be starting to become a threat for them.

Or, if your child is delaying doing their homework and is wanting to keep playing computer games instead, you might discuss with them whether their balance of soothing strategies and drives is right, and that they might need to increase their drives a bit more – then challenge them as to how they can do that.

The key is to help your child start to learn about getting the right level of drives, in order to gain a positive sense of achievement and success – but not so many that they become overly tired or stressed, and shift into a threat system. And to support your child in learning the importance of soothing activities, to manage their drives and threats successfully.

The three systems also give you a common, 'safe' language to use with your child, so that you can talk about their critical mind moments in a way that feels validating to them, but which doesn't necessarily imply that their critical mind was true.

For example, if your child was to say, 'I'm an idiot. Everyone thinks I'm dumb,' you could then reflect back that it sounds like they are in a threat place right now, which must be very tricky and stressful for them.

Once your child is more of an expert on the three systems approach, you can then support them as they develop this knowledge to help them in their day-to-day life, which we will now explore.

Promoting soothing activities in everyday life

We all have activities that help to soothe us when we are stressed and allow us to relax and recover from the day. If you look back to Chapter 2, Worksheet 8, you spotted the different strategies you use to promote your soothing system. We need to do the same with your children, to ensure they are having sufficient downtime to manage the demands of their life and have the energy to deal with any threats that emerge.

Look back at Chapter 4, Worksheets 23 and 24, where you jotted down ways your child's soothing system is activated. It can be helpful to chat to your child about these strategies and encourage them to incorporate them into their daily life.

Getting into a drive system

Some children find it hard to shift into a drive state in order to gain the necessary motivation to undertake their academic work, chores, or even enjoyable activities that could give them a sense of achievement. It can be useful to explore strategies with your child to help them get into an effective drive system. These will be individual to your child, depending on their personality and interests. Ideas to try are:

1.   Music

Music can inspire and energise people and shift them into an achieving state of mind. You could explore this with your child, taking celebrity examples to build up your message. For example, the New Zealand rugby team, who use a haka to get into the right mindset for their rugby games. Serena Williams has also spoken about the 'pump-up' music she always listens to before walking on to a tennis court. Many runners listen to music as a way to motivate themselves to keep going. You could discuss with your child whether there are any songs or music pieces they could play, to get them positively energised and into a drive state.

2.   Cheerleading themselves

Back in Chapter 3, on page 60, we explored the benefits of cheerleading ourselves as parents to help us feel more ready to face a parenting challenge. The same is true with young people. If they can say the right things to themselves before undertaking work, it can increase the chance that they get going with the work. Take this example:

Example

Sarah is eleven and has history homework that needs to be completed by the end of the day.

Sarah's demotivated voice: 'History is sooo boring. This is going to take for ever and be painful to do.'

Sarah's cheerleading voice: 'I've got this. Let's crack on with it and get it over with. The sooner it's done, the better!'

Compare Sarah's two inner voices. Which one do you think is most helpful, to ensure she shifts into a drive state and undertakes the work?

You can chat to your child about cheerleading themselves into a drive system. It may be helpful for them to write out general cheerleading statements and to keep them somewhere useful, to remind themselves, such as:

•   Displayed on their bedroom wall or pin board

•   Written as a note or screensaver on their mobile phone

- As a note in their pencil case

- Represented by a poster or picture

3. 'Reverse laziness'

Reverse laziness is a concept we sometimes discuss with our families to explore the strategy of clearing work as quickly as possible in order to then relax in a soothing activity. The idea of reverse laziness is that we believe we are truly lazy people – when we are in a soothing moment, we want to be fully in this system – relaxing as much as possible, without any chores or work hanging over us, which otherwise gives us a low-level threat throughout the relaxing period and thus takes away some of the joy of the soothing activity.

Up until undertaking the work or the chore, most people have a niggly threat feeling, constantly present to some degree. Therefore, in an attempt to remove the threat and maximise the soothing time, the best philosophy is to undertake the work or chore *as soon as you possibly can*.

On the face of it, you look incredibly diligent and conscientious, but actually the goal is to try to bring forward the soothing system to as early a time as you can, and then have the joy of doing so, free of work hanging over you – thus maximising your laziness.

This can be a helpful philosophy to explain to young people and children. It also has the helpful side effect that you need to remind them to undertake work much less often.

Your child managing their own threat system

We all have threats at times and our children are no exception. We will not be able to completely protect them from threats in life – although the threats can be minimised if we support our children to get the balance right between drives and soothing activities. However, our main goals as parents are twofold:

1. To help our children learn how to shift out of a threat to the best of their ability

2. To support our children in developing a compassionate rather than a critical mind when experiencing a threat

We will now explore each of these goals in turn, in order to ensure your child is prepared for when their threat system is triggered.

Helping our children shift out of a threat system

When in a stressful threat state, it can be hard for our brains to shift into gear and work out how to make us feel better. This is hard enough for adults to do and even more difficult for children, particularly achieving these skills with some level of independence from us. Therefore, it can be helpful to have a few strategies 'ready to go', so they don't need to work out what to do when they find themselves in a threat state.

Ideas that are worth trying:

1. Calming box

Use a shoe box or other container and, with your child, agree on a few objects to place inside it that your child could calm themselves with when their threat system is triggered. These objects should not be the toys and objects they play with every day but rather things that are *only* to be played with when your child is in a threat state.

These items could include:

- fidget spinners and other fidget toys

- bubbles

- a cuddly toy

- bubble wrap to pop

- a note from you encouraging them through it

- putty or slime

- colouring-in books and new felt-tip pens or pencils

- a calming book

- photographs that soothe your child

- a toy or book linked to their special interest

- sensory toys

You and your child can then agree on where the calming box should be placed in your house, and whether or not you, as a parent, are allowed to prompt your child to take five minutes out with their calming box when their threat system has been triggered. Some young people can take this direction without issue, but for other children, a verbal prompt to go to their calming box can escalate their threat system. Such children either need a visual prompt (such as you showing them a photograph of their calming box or making a hand gesture that symbolises the calming box), or you staying completely quiet. Therefore, it is helpful to have a plan in advance about how the calming box should be used.

2.   Planning sheet

If some threats regularly crop up, you could work with your child to develop a written plan to manage that threat. This could include:

- Before the challenge

- During the challenge

- After the challenge

Example

Haro has autism and ADHD. He finds that he keeps forgetting items when he packs his school bag each morning. Haro has been in trouble a few times with teachers for forgetting his homework and other items, like his PE kit. The result of this is that Haro becomes stressed on school mornings, often has lunch-time detentions, and gets into arguments with his parents. But now Haro has developed the following plan with the help of his dad.

My school bag plan	
The night before school, I will:	<ul><li>Take out my school books from today and put them on my shelf</li><li>Put my new school books into my bag</li><li>Check my Google Classroom for homework due in tomorrow</li></ul>

	• Make sure I've got all the home-work packed in my bag • Leave my lunchbox and water bottle in the kitchen • Put a plastic bag on top of my school bag, ready for my PE kit • Check my homework diary for extra stuff I need to pack
On a school morning, I will:	• Collect my lunchbox and filled water bottle from the kitchen worksurface (Mum will sort these out for me) • Put my PE kit in the plastic bag (remember my trainers!)
Every Friday night, I will:	• Put my PE kit in the wash
Every Sunday night, I will:	• Write into my homework diary any extra stuff I need to remember for the next week. Think: my trombone, football matches, school trip money, etc.

As Haro took ownership of this plan and decided what to pack and when, he was much keener to stick to it, which helped shift the arguments with his parents. He also decided to stick the plan on the back of his bedroom door, to help him remember it. In addition, Haro stopped getting into trouble at school about forgotten items, so packing his school bag no longer triggered his threat system.

When supporting your child to devise such a planning sheet, it is useful to act as the co-pilot rather than the main pilot – allowing them to decide on the plan whenever possible and to feel in control of what they do. You could then spend time reflecting with them on how they will remember to use this planning sheet and praise them for coming up with all their ideas.

3.   Replaying a video of themselves dealing with a threat

When in a threat state, children often feel they can't cope with a challenge, and that it's too hard for them – even when they've managed that situation in the past. You could find that no amount of you reminding them that they were OK before helps your child shift out of their threat system.

This is where filming comes in – videoing your child just after they've managed to cope with a threat (while they still have a sense of achievement for surviving it) can be a useful tool, as you can then replay it to them when they are considering re-entering a similar situation in the future.

Example

Nine-year-old Iman was very anxious about joining a girls-only football club one Saturday morning and struggled to separate from her dad to join the practice. After about forty-five minutes of trying, Iman eventually managed to join in with a couple of football drills and started to enjoy herself. She later took part in a mini match at the end of the practice, kicking the ball to a fellow team member, which resulted in a goal being scored. Iman's dad filmed a mini interview with Iman on his iPhone as soon as she came off the pitch, asking her how much fun she'd had and whether it would be worth beating the anxiety next week to join in with the football practice. Iman answered enthusiastically and told her future self to get onto the pitch as soon as possible next Saturday, to maximise her play time.

The following week, Iman had similar anxieties about taking part in the football club activities and became tearful. However, watching the mini interview of herself on her dad's phone made her smile and increased her confidence to give the practice a go.

4.   Encouraging your child to undertake a self-soothing activity to beat the threats

In Chapter 5, we explored the actions you can undertake to help soothe your children's systems, including:

- Supporting your child yourself

- Using your child's senses and focus of attention

- Breathing exercises – soothing rhythmic breathing

- Muscle relaxation

- Thinking of feelings as waves

Over time, you will gain a sense of which of these strategies is most effective for your child and they should also become more confident about using them. You can then support your child to start doing their favourite strategies as soon as they spot that they need to – without you having to be close by. Again, it can be helpful for your child to make a reminder about which strategy they will try and when. You can then praise and reward them afterwards for putting the strategies in place.

It can also be helpful to pull together a plan to support your child to promote their soothing activities, encourage their drives and support them in managing their threats. Look back over the suggestions in the previous few pages of this chapter, and complete Worksheet 35:

Worksheet 35: My plan to support my child with the three systems

Helping them to promote soothing activities:

Best ways to get them into a drive state:

Ideas to help my child manage their threats:

We have looked at all the different ways we can help our children manage when their threat system is triggered. However, it is also important to support our children to deal with their critical minds and, ideally, begin to develop their own compassionate mind from as young an age as possible. Therefore, we will now move on to this goal.

Introducing a compassionate approach to your child

Initially, we need to introduce our children to the idea of how important it is to use a compassionate rather than a critical mind, and the positive impact this can have on our lives. One way to introduce this concept is to compare and contrast two made-up adult figures with your child – one who has a critical approach and the other who has a compassionate approach. For example:

Rock-climbing example

Let's imagine that you absolutely love rock climbing and you are naturally good at it. You decide to join a rock-climbing club to progress with your rock-climbing skills, in the hope that one day you will be able to join the national rock-climbing squad. You visit two different rock-climbing clubs.

Club 1: You meet the instructor, Joe, who shows you the facilities and tells you about the club. As you are looking around, Joe suddenly yells at a child who is having a rock-climbing lesson. He shouts, 'Oy, Freya! What on earth are you doing?! That's rubbish climbing . . . haven't I told you a hundred times before to not support all your weight with your hands? Are you stupid or something? You know you have to find ways to support your weight with your feet, too. You'll never get to the top!'

Club 2: You then move to the second club, where you meet an instructor called Jason. Jason shows you the facilities at the club, which are fairly similar to Club 1. While you're looking around, Jason spots a child having a lesson who seems to be having the same issues as the child from Club 1. Jason also calls over to the child, saying, 'Hey, Sophie! Remember what we said about trying to support your weight with your feet as well as your hands. I can see you're struggling a bit with this skill, aren't you? Not to worry – everyone finds it hard to begin with. I'm sure you'll get it, but I think perhaps you need a bit more time working on it. I'll come and help after I've finished my meeting.'

You can then discuss with your child which rock-climbing club they would pick and talk through why they've chosen that club. Children generally pick Club 2, as the end result is the same for both Freya and Sophie (e.g. becoming more skilful at rock climbing). However, it is clear that the process of becoming a better rock climber will be much nicer at Club 2 than at Club 1.

From this example, you can then explain to your child how everyone has a critical mind in their heads – just like the instructor, Joe, at Club 1 – which tends to make us feel bad. However, we don't need to listen to this critical instructor in our heads and it is OK to instead develop a more compassionate mind, just like the instructor, Jason, at Club 2.

Compassionate mind superhero

Many children have wonderful imaginations and regularly invent games or stories in their play. For children who love a fantasy world, it can be helpful for them to develop a character connected to their compassionate mind.

For example, their compassionate mind might be a superhero, who can fly into their minds and save them from the critical mind by telling them the truth about what's going on.

Their compassionate mind might be an imaginary friend, who can talk to them in a calm and kind manner and stick up for them when their critical mind is being mean.

Their compassionate mind might be an animal, such as a wise owl, which swoops in to difficult situations to use kind words to support them in their battle with their critical mind.

Or their compassionate mind might be an angel on one shoulder, who helps them to stand up to the devil on the other shoulder, who is the critical mind.

If your child enjoys engaging in such imaginative storytelling, then you can take the lead from them to gain more detail about their compassionate-mind character. You can discuss with your child:

- What this character looks like. They might want to draw or paint a picture of this character to make it come to life more easily

- The tone of voice and facial expressions the character uses when speaking to them (remembering what we explored in Chapter 3 about the need for a neutral facial expression, plus a calm, non-judgemental voice tone)

- This character's wisdom, in knowing the truth about tricky situations, as it can see the whole picture of what is going on, rather than just the negative view of the critical mind. This character's wisdom also understands the critical mind's intentions, but finds other ways to achieve these intentions in a more compassionate way

- The courage and strength of this character – ready to stand up to the critical mind whenever it needs to, however hard that might be in the moment

- The character's caring nature, which uses supportive and kind words

Depending on your child's interests and personality, you might like to bring competition into their compassionate mind character. For example, you could talk to your child about how the compassionate mind is a superhero, who can defeat the critical-mind character. It can also be useful to keep a tally of the 'wins'.

Compassionate mind characteristics

If your child is less keen on imaginative exercises, it is still helpful to draw out the key characteristics of their compassionate mind, including the three areas we have discussed before:

- The wisdom of the compassionate mind, whether this is your child stepping back in their minds and working out the best way forward during difficult moments – based on all of the facts, including the original intentions of the critical mind. Or using their wisdom to appreciate that this moment is hard for them, and that is OK and normal

- The strength of their compassionate mind to have the courage not to be overwhelmed by difficult and distressing moments, but instead to strive to act differently

- The commitment to taking the most caring and healthy path possible, even when other paths might feel easier in that moment

Practising using a compassionate mind (1)

By this point, your child is probably becoming more familiar with their compassionate mind – whether as an imaginative superhero character or as a part of their own brain, designed to help them stand up to their inner critical mind when times are tough. Now we need to encourage your child to try to connect with their compassionate mind during a difficult moment. Again, it can be helpful for you to take a 'co-piloting' role when your child is first attempting this skill, in order to prompt them to try it out and perhaps to remind them of the types of words they need to use.

Example

Thirteen-year-old Megan started feeling stressed when attempting some difficult mathematics home-work and her mum discovered Megan becoming tearful at her desk.

Megan (tearful): 'I can't do this algebra. It's impossible! I'll never be able to do it. It's stupid and impossible, and I can't do it.'

Mum: 'It looks like these sums are really tricky and they're upsetting you lots, aren't they?'

Megan (shouting): 'They're awful! I can't do them. I'm so stupid at algebra. I'll never be able to get it. I'm such an idiot. I hate this!'

Mum: 'Oh, Megan. And one of the worst parts is that this homework seems to have made that critical devil of yours start to say mean stuff about how good you are at mathematics.'

Megan (tearful): 'I know! But it's just so hard to believe I'm any good when I can't get my head around this stupid homework.'

Mum: 'And I'm sure your critical devil loves this type of tricky homework, too. It probably gives it a really good excuse to lay into you and be mean to you.'

Megan (less tearful): 'Yes! It's stupid, too. I hate it.'

Mum: 'I'm wondering, Megan. Maybe this is a good time for you to remember that kind angel (Megan's name for her compassionate mind) of yours? What would she say to you?'

Megan (grumpy): 'I don't know! Something about how this year's work is a step up from last year's work.'

Mum: 'Do you know what, I think you're right. I reckon that's exactly the sort of thing the kind angel would say. Maybe it's worth taking five minutes out of this homework, just to connect with that kind angel of yours, as I reckon the critical devil is stopping your mind from working as well as it normally does, making the homework even harder to do. What do you think?'

Megan (sighing): 'OK, Mum.'

As you can see from Megan's case study, Megan was initially not in a place where she could easily connect with her compassionate mind and it wasn't at the front of her memory. However, her mum's approach of acknowledging Megan's anger and upset feelings, and then gently mentioning her critical mind, allowed Megan to stand back from her emotions to some extent, to remember the power of the critical mind, and the potential for her to be more compassionate to herself.

Once our children are ready to connect with their compassionate mind, it can be helpful for them to calm their body and mind down, using one of the techniques you identified in Worksheet 23, page 84.

Example

Mum: 'Right, why don't you start by doing that slow breathing technique?'

Megan: 'I know, Mum! The one where I slow my breathing down a bit and breathe in and out like that for about a minute. You don't need to remind me, Mum. I've got this.'

Mum: 'OK, Megan . . . over to you.'

Megan does her rhythmic breathing for a minute, with her eyes closed.

In Megan's example, you can see how she will now be in a better state to connect with her compassionate mind – much more so than when her mum first discovered her, when she had heightened stress about the homework. Let's follow Megan's journey to the next stage, when she can connect with her compassionate mind:

Example

Megan: 'That breathing is always relaxing, Mum.'

Mum: 'I bet it is, Megan. Now, remember to think about what your lovely, kind angel would say to you about this algebra homework.'

Megan: 'Yes, she'd tell me that it's really very tricky and that, probably, most people in my class will be struggling with it, too.'

Mum: 'I'm sure they are. And what does that kind angel of yours think about how you're doing?'

Megan: 'She can see how hard I'm trying and that it's not my fault I can't do it. It's just I haven't got my head around it yet, so it's fighting with me.'

Mum: 'That's it! And does your kind angel blame you?'

Megan: 'No! Of course not, Mum. She knows I'm normally good at this subject and is telling me that maybe I'm being a bit impatient with the work – that I'll get it in the end.'

Mum: 'Your kind angel sounds very wise.'

Megan: 'She is. I think I know what to do now, Mum.'

Mum: 'What's that, Megan?'

Megan: 'I think I'm going to get a drink, and then come back to this, watch the help video again, and see if I can figure it out. If I can't, I'm ringing Anna; she's great with this stuff.'

Mum: 'That sounds like a sensible plan, Megan. How are you feeling about it now?'

Megan: 'Fine, Mum, honestly. You don't need to make a fuss, you know.'

Mum: 'I know, Megan. It sounds like you've got this.'

This example shows how Megan could imagine the words of her kind angel and these words helped her to know what she should do next. It is helpful for you to support your child in imagining how their compassionate mind would view the threat situation they're in. It may be that your child can do this independently once they've used one of their strategies to regulate their emotions. However, you may initially need to support your child by asking them questions that will bring out their compassionate mind more clearly, like Megan's mum did.

Practising using a compassionate mind: with EASE (2)

In order to engage with our compassionate minds, we need to be able to step back from our thoughts, feelings and intentions (including our critical mind's viewpoint), and recognise that this is not beneficial to us, then figure out what a more compassionate approach would be. Many youngsters find using the EASE framework helps them to do this, going through each of the four steps to help them and then use their compassionate mind effectively. Writing it down can be useful to allow your child to step back and see the whole situation on paper rather than trying to hold it in their minds. Therefore, it may be beneficial to encourage your child to complete the following log, based on EASE, to support them in practising using their compassionate mind.

My compassionate mind log				
Situation:				
Emotions	Critical mind	Actions to soothe myself	Stopping with compassion	Emotions now?

Here is Megan's completed compassionate mind log to show what your child might write in each column.

My compassionate mind log				
Situation: Impossible homework				
Emotions	Critical mind	Actions to soothe myself	Stopping with compassion	Emotions now?
Upset Frustrated Annoyed	I'll never be any good at algebra I'm too stupid	Chilled out breaths for one minute	This is really hard and at a much higher level than I'm used to Of course I'm finding it tough. I've only just started this type of algebra Don't forget that I'm pretty good at mathematics, so I'm bound to get it in the end	Still a bit frustrated More relaxed about it though

Practising using a compassionate mind (3)

It can be really helpful to support your child to practise engaging with their compassionate mind when they are in a calm place, so they become better able to do so during difficult moments. Therefore, you can try to:

1. Encourage your child to stand in front of a mirror and talk to themselves the way they would speak to a good friend. Chat to them about how it feels to use this compassionate voice to themselves and whether or not it's a helpful approach

2. Suggest to your child that they write a list of their own achievements and then ask them to read the list out loud to themselves – allowing time for each one to sink in

3. Undertake drama exercises with your child. You can pick a threat situation together and then encourage your child to first talk about it as if they were their critical mind. Then ask your child

to talk about it from their compassionate mind. Together, you can review how each version felt and which felt better for them

Through these exercises, your child should start to learn the value of adopting a compassionate mind. However, they may initially struggle to do so, finding the critical mind more automatic, if it's been around for a long time. This is where it can be helpful to discuss with your child the helpfulness of 'faking it until you make it'.

Faking it until you make it

When we try a compassionate mind approach after our threat system has been triggered, it can feel strange at first, although this feeling of strangeness tends to reduce with time.

It may be useful to chat to your child about how they may initially need to go through the motions of using a compassionate mind, even if it does not feel natural to start with. Dr Mary Welford describes this as chatting to your child about stepping into, 'the version of themselves that they want to become'. An alternative way of doing this is to describe it as your child 'faking it until they make it'. You can then use examples of celebrities your child is familiar with.

For example, Beyoncé has discussed her alter ego 'Sasha Fierce', whom she adopts to give her the confidence, glamour and energy she needs to sing in front of thousands of people on stage.

Katy Perry has also been open about her lack of confidence when she first started out as a singer. She needed to fake confidence to get into the correct headspace to stand up on stage in front of a huge audience.

In summary

It can be of great benefit to start building your child's compassionate mind so that they can develop their resilient, strong and supportive inner voice from a young age, to protect them as they journey through life. In order to do this, we need to:

- Teach our children about the three emotional regulation systems

- Help them to have the right number of soothing activities in their lives

- Support our children to activate their drive systems when necessary

- Help our children manage threats

- Develop our children's compassionate mind, ensuring we introduce this concept in a way they understand, using creative and imaginative techniques, if helpful

- Help our children to practise connecting with their compassionate mind. We can do this through our direct guidance, by encouraging them to use the EASE framework and to use logs, and sometimes by encouraging them to 'fake it until they make it', until it becomes more natural

7 Compassionate Parenting in Action

In Chapter 7, we include examples of how a compassionate parenting approach can be used to deal with various parenting problems. These might be useful to look at if you are struggling with a similar problem (although you will need to tailor your compassionate parenting approach depending on the formulations you have completed for your child from Chapter 4).

My child won't share his toys

We have an expectation that from an early age our children will share their toys when prompted to do so. Parents often feel great pressure for this to occur – particularly when children start going to nursery school or have playdates with other children. Therefore, if our children don't share their toys readily with others, it can feel awkward and quickly becomes a threat for us.

However, sharing is a developmental skill that children learn over time and you will probably need to shape your parenting approach depending on the age of your child.

It is helpful to remember the EASE strategy when managing moments when your child is not sharing their toys to the extent that you (or someone with you) feels they should be.

The first step, 'E', is to spot the **Emotions** in yourself as a parent that are being triggered by your child's seeming lack of sharing, and how these impact upon your thoughts, your memories linked to the situation, how your body feels, and the actions you are tempted to do in that moment. Common emotions include:

embarrassment	anxiety
shame	stress
guilt	frustration
anger	despair

If these emotions take over, it will be more challenging for you to manage this parenting situation in a compassionate way. Therefore, if you spot these emotions around, it is helpful to undertake the 'A' step, taking an **action to soothe** yourself.

For example, it may be helpful to:

1. Take a few rhythmic deep breaths or take another soothing action before starting the parenting intervention

2. Remember any relevant cheerleading sentences to help ready yourself for talking to your child about sharing

3. Use your compassionate mind to remind yourself that your child does not yet know how to share, and that this is a skill they are still in the process of developing. Hold this in mind in an accepting way, knowing that your child will master this skill, but they just need a little bit more time and practice in order to do so. Therefore, it is understandable if your child feels unable to share their toys with others. You will remain committed to helping them with sharing over the next few months and years

4. Be mindful of your voice tone, body posture and facial expressions when explaining to your child about the need to share

Following the EASE strategy, we now move on to the 'S' stage of **stopping with compassion.** It is important to tailor your parenting strategies to your child's age, as their ability to share will depend on how old they are at the time.

Under threes

Before the age of three, children simply do not have the ability to fully understand or undertake sharing. Therefore, it is helpful to approach sharing with young children from a compassionate place:

Parenting ideas to try:

It may be helpful to explain to your child the reason the other child would like to have a turn with their toys.

You could calmly and quietly count down with your child from a number you think they understand (e.g. ten slow seconds), while another child is having a turn playing with a desired toy. Once you have counted this time down, it is your child's turn with the toy (then count down the same time until it is the other child's turn again, etc.).

Recognising how hard sharing is at this age, you could attempt to distract your child or the other child with another toy – talking enthusiastically about its merits.

You could also clearly but kindly explain to the other child that it is your child's turn with this toy, but as soon as they have finished with it then the other child can play with it for as long as they want.

Four- to five-year-olds

When aged around four to five years old, our children start to know the social expectations they should share and they can also fulfil these expectations under certain situations. However, it can be very hard for them to control their impulses not to share at other times.

Dr James Kirby and his colleagues have researched the boundaries of children's compassion and sharing at four to five years old and found that when children didn't lose anything important by sharing (e.g. the chance to complete a task and gain a sticker), then they were more likely to share some of their own resources. The four- to five-year-olds were also more likely to share if they were given an explicit instruction to do so. However, if there was a personal cost to the children for sharing (e.g. not getting a sticker for completing a task), then the children were much less likely to show compassion and share. And competitiveness further turned off the children's openness to sharing. This is helpful research to remember, as it can shape our compassionate parenting approach to supporting our four- to five-year-olds to learn how to share.

Parenting ideas to try:

You could explain to your child the reason the other child would like to have a turn with their toys. If you decide that your child needs to share a toy, then think about how to reduce the personal cost to your child. For example, is there another toy or activity you could suggest, that would help them manage their difficult emotions more easily?

Then, give them a clear and direct instruction to share their toy, as this can make it easier for them to do so.

Avoid any element of competition with the toys to be shared as well.

Six years and older

From six years old, children are developmentally more able to share. However, some children still find sharing a difficult thing to do consistently.

Parenting ideas to try:

You will be an expert on your child by this age and so, depending on your knowledge of what works best for them, you could reflect with your child that they seem to be struggling to share their toys and ask them if that's the case. Then spend time discussing whether they have any ideas as to how to solve this problem and how you can support them in doing so.

You could calmly but clearly tell your child that they need to share their toys – explaining the reasons why they need to share, if this would be helpful to them. A countdown can additionally help your child mentally prepare to share their toy – for example, by saying, 'After ten seconds, you need to pass the toy over,' and then slowly counting down from ten.

Show clear pride and positivity when your child does share their toy – letting them see it as a good experience. This can work even before your child has handed over the toy. For example, by stating, 'I am so proud of you for sharing that toy . . .', and pausing in silence, waiting for your child to hand it over. Once they do so, you can then repeat the praise.

The last stage of EASE is relooking at your '**E**' **emotions now.** It can be helpful to review these questions:

- How did you get on with managing your child's difficult sharing moment?

- Has there been a change in the emotions that were initially triggered? If yes, has your mind also changed (such as your thoughts, inner critical voice and memories)?

- Do you need to take any more 'A' actions to soothe to help yourself with these emotions?

- Have you learnt anything helpful from the episode that will be useful to remember when your child next has difficulty sharing? If so, how can you remember this learning?

My plan for managing my child's sharing difficulties:

'E': What emotions do I expect I will be feeling?

'A': What actions can I use that will best soothe me?

'S': How can I stop with compassion, to support my child and me through this?

'E': How am I hoping to feel by the end?

(I can also note down any learning I make here)

My child keeps having toileting accidents in the day

It can be very difficult if your child has a longstanding issue with toileting – whether they struggle to stay dry at night or have urine or faeces accidents during the daytime. There can be a number of reasons for this, including:

- Pressure: parents often feel great pressure for their children to be 100% toilet trained by the time they start at nursery school or reception – at three to four years old. However, this simply isn't possible for some children, despite their parents' best efforts

- Biology: toilet training involves certain biological systems working in the correct way, which isn't always the case. For example, some children's bowels just seem to be slower to process faeces and are more prone to constipation than others. Another example is that, by around seven years old, most children produce enough of a chemical called vasopressin at night to help keep them dry until morning. But for other children, this system isn't fully up and running until several years later. A final example is that autistic children can often struggle to recognise their internal body sensations, so they are more at risk of missing the signals that they need the toilet. Parents can end up feeling helpless when there is an underlying biological reason for their child's toileting issue that they can't easily resolve themselves

- Practicalities: unfortunately, toileting difficulties can result in significant practical issues, too. A parent may need to bring additional bedding, pyjamas and absorbent pads for their child if they are staying away. Plus, there will be more washing, given the additional bed linen that needs cleaning. Toileting accidents during the day can make a trip out the house much more difficult, too, as parents may need to plan toilet stops, bring spare underclothes, work out how to store soiled clothes, etc. Not forgetting that some accidents can result in children smelling, which can cause further stress, as we are motivated to protect our children from the negative judgements of others. Such practical issues have resulted in some of the families we see in clinic feeling unable to leave the house unless it is absolutely necessary to do so, which can cause further problems, such as isolation and loneliness

In light of these factors, it is little wonder that toileting difficulties can quickly become threats to parents. Therefore, it is beneficial to use the EASE compassionate parenting strategy.

When a parent discovers another wet bed or other accident, it is understandable that this can result in the parent experiencing a wide range of emotions, such as:

Frustration: that an accident has happened again

Sadness: that their child has not overcome the toileting issue, which they as parents are still coping with

Anxiety: wondering whether this will be with their child for ever

Fear: that their child will be bullied by others who notice the accidents

Anger: at the unfairness of still having to manage toileting difficulties when others don't

Guilt: feeling as if you 'should' have resolved this issue by now but are unable to do so

The first step of EASE is looking at '**E' emotions** to work out whether you are experiencing one or more of these difficult emotions and considering how strong the feeling is in that moment, and the impact that emotion is having on you.

Next is the '**A' action to soothe**. This involves thinking compassionately about yourself as the parent, needing to deal with this toileting difficulty.

What do you need to do to help manage your difficult emotion(s)?

Think about the soothing actions that would best help you in this moment. It may be that taking deep breaths allows you to regain a sense of control. Or imagining your child in ten years' time, nappy-free and carefree with their toileting, and you no longer having to think about accidents.

It may be useful to connect with the reasons behind your child's toileting difficulties – particularly if there is an underlying biological issue that makes toileting much harder for them.

You may also need a more practical strategy, such as working with a partner, so that one of you deals with the practical side of cleaning up the accident and the other one focuses on your child, keeping them as relaxed as possible and experiencing the warmth of your parenting, even at this stressful time.

We can now move on to the **'S'** of **stopping with compassion**.

Should your critical mind be present during such accidents, it is important to connect with the intention of that critical voice before you start introducing new parental strategies. Why is it giving you a tough time about this difficult toileting moment?

Perhaps your critical mind is trying to drive you into resolving the toileting issue as soon as possible. Or is it attempting to make you feel bad, to ease the feelings of parental guilt. If you are able to work out the critical mind's intentions, it can be beneficial to directly act on your discoveries. For example:

Intention of critical voice	Examples of a more compassionate response
Trying to speed up sorting out the toileting issue	Recognise the impact this issue is having in a way that is kinder to yourself
	Connect with your wisdom in reminding yourself that the accidents will take time to sort out. Acknowledge that you are not purposefully delaying how long it is taking to resolve them. In fact, you are already very motivated to stop the accidents from happening. It's just proving difficult right now
	Make a commitment to undertaking some more practical steps to help move forwards with resolving the accidents. But recognise

	that you can't do anything until you have finished the necessary clean-up process first. And thus, undertaking this in a compassionate and accepting manner is probably the most helpful action you can take in this moment, for yourself and your child
Trying to make you feel bad to help with parental guilt	Accept that you feel guilty about this issue, as the guilt is a response of your natural caring and protective side – your desire to 'take this issue away' for your child, so it no longer impacts on their lives. Acknowledge the actions you have used so far and that you have been trying to help
	Consider the reasons for the toileting issue and that there is no 'fault' or 'blame', just an unlucky combination of events
	Think about what other, more active ideas you could try that might help move things forward, so you no longer feel as bad
Mirroring negative comments you have heard from the people around you (e.g. criticising your parenting)	Connect with the fact that being a parent is a hard job, but you are doing the best you can
	Reflect that nobody is 100% perfect all the time, especially not in parenting. In fact, it is normal to get some things wrong at times
	Think of a cheerleading statement that focuses on your skills as a parent
	Take time to consider what motivates the people around you to be critical of you – is it 'your stuff' or 'their stuff'?
	Work out if there is another trusted person in your life who you could ask to tell you how they view your parenting, and who you know will give you a more balanced view

When discussing accidents or toileting difficulties with your child, it is important to consider your voice tone, body language and facial expressions during the conversation. What would be the most helpful in this situation? (You can note down any thoughts under the 'S' section in the planning table at the end of this section). We will focus on ideas for daytime accidents in this chapter, but if you are struggling with night-time accidents, please do consider the listed 'next steps' resources at the bottom of this section to gain more support on resolving them.

Parenting ideas to try for daytime accidents:

The goal of these ideas is to keep our 'wisdom' of the nature of childhood to heart, by trying to use a creative or playful approach to parenting strategies as often as we can. This will help ensure that our children stay engaged in the work and do not experience a critical parenting voice, but rather the more protective, compassionate parenting voice.

1. Use a playful approach to explore whether your child knows when they need to use the toilet. For example:

Using a big piece of paper, have your child lie on the paper and draw around their body. Then get your child to draw onto the body picture where they feel the sensations of needing the toilet	Read books together that discuss the body's sensations of needing to go to the loo
Act out together the different signs that your child needs the toilet. For example, both sitting on your feet pretending to need the loo, or walking while crossing legs over, etc. (these actions may well be unique to your child)	Draw out a thermometer scale and discuss how the body sensations increase in 'temperature' from being 'cool' (not very strong sensations) all the way to being 'boiling hot' (when your child is about to have an accident)
Discuss with your child the signs that *you* need the toilet and talk about them just before you go to the toilet yourself	

2. It can be helpful to act out with your child them pretending to use the toilet when feeling these sensations. For example, the two of you initially playing together in your house and then your child pretending they have spotted needing the toilet (telling you the signs they need it). Then going to the toilet and acting out using it (some children love being noisy while pretending to use the toilet!). If your child likes competitions, you could challenge them to 'timed trials', to race to the toilet as quickly as they can, while you time them, from different rooms in your house. You can then keep track of the times and see if they can 'beat the clock' when they are actually needing the toilet.

3. Make your toilet as 'child friendly' as possible. For example, you can:

    *   Put your child's pictures up on the wall

    *   Buy novelty toilet paper

    *   Buy a novelty toilet seat

    *   Have a box with toys/books just for the bathroom

    *   Have a stool for your child's feet

    *   Have a blanket to place over their lap if they dislike the cold while on the toilet

4. Make up a story with your child about their wee or poo, to help motivate them to use the toilet rather than having an accident. This idea was first introduced in 1983 by Terry Heins and Karen Ritchie. The child's poo was called 'Sneaky Poo' and the authors used Sneaky Poo to help children understand their poo accidents, and what to do about it. It can be useful to let your child come up with a name for their wees or poos themselves and develop a story together. For example:

    *   'Bob the poo', who wants to go down the toilet to find his poo family and have a party with them

- 'The poop monster', who needs to be beaten by being sent down the loo

- 'My inside tap', which turns on too quickly when I'm not on the toilet

Your child can draw pictures or help you write out a story about their wee or poo characters, including how they are going to beat them, to help reinforce a change in behaviour.

5.   Reward systems can be very helpful. However, these should not be used to reward clean pants, as children who have constipation can end up holding on to their poos for longer, rather than letting them pass out, which can actually worsen the constipation. Instead, they should be used to reward using the toilet well. Reward systems might include:

Stickers for a wee or poo in the toilet	Marbles in a jar each time the toilet is used well
A bead on a piece of string – and when the string is full of beads, the child can trade it in for a reward	A 'lucky dip' bag of cheap toys each time the child uses the toilet well
Colouring in a section of a picture – and when the picture is fully coloured, the child gets a reward	An instant food 'treat' after using the toilet well (e.g. a Smartie, a Jelly Tot or a handful of grapes). This treat food cannot be given at other times initially, to make it more special

6. The clean-up – It can be helpful for your child to be involved in the clean-up after an accident. However, it is important to approach this in a compassionate manner with a matter-of-fact voice tone, rather than an angry, punishing voice tone. The goal of helping with the clean-up is to link an accident with the sense of there being some low-level hassle for your child, so they learn that it is easier and quicker to just use the toilet. Plus, it ensures your child knows the independence skills that allow them to appropriately use the toilet (e.g. wiping their own bottom). You can choose the level of clean-up that you think is most appropriate for your child knowing their age and ability in this area. But it might involve any of the following:

- Your child letting any soiled poo fall in the toilet from off their underwear

- Your child putting their underwear into a special place (e.g. a special laundry box or the washing machine)

- Your child having a shower if they are very messy

- Your child wiping their own bottom

- Your child collecting fresh underwear to wear

7. Make sure you have all the 'basics' in place. For example:

- Encouraging your child to drink regularly. This is very important if they are suffering from constipation to soften their poos, but it is also key for daytime wetters, to ensure they have plenty of practice using the toilet correctly

- Ensure your child has fibre in their diet if they suffer from constipation. For example, dried fruit (like dried mango, apricots and raisins), whole grains, nuts (if they don't have a nut allergy), beans and pulses, and potatoes with skins

- Exercise is very good for stimulating the bowel and reducing the risk of constipation. Plus, there is good evidence to show that exercise can have a positive impact on stress, which is helpful to your child, as toileting issues can naturally cause stress and, in turn, stress can sometimes increase the rate of toileting accidents

The last step of EASE is to relook at your '**E' emotions now**, to see how you have got on with managing a specific accident, or more generally with your child's toileting issues. You can ask yourself:

- Has there been a change in the emotions that were initially triggered?

- Do I need to take any more 'A' actions to soothe to help myself with these emotions and their impact on my mind?

- Have I learnt anything helpful from the episode that will be useful to remember when my child next has an accident when I am encouraging good toilet use? If so, how can I remember this learning?

You may see from your review of emotions now that your difficult emotions are still fairly high, even if you have attempted the stopping with compassion actions, because you are continuing to find it hard to shift your child's toileting difficulties. This can be more likely to occur if your child has an underlying biological issue that contributes to their toileting difficulty, or there is another important, relevant issue (e.g. a significant fear of using the toilet, or an upcoming significant life event for your child, like a house move). Therefore, it may be that you need to gain additional, external help to further shift your child's toileting behaviour, such as:

Next steps

Talk to your health visitor service if your child is under five.

Look up the ERIC website (as listed at the end of the book) which has a list of online resources and books that can help with toileting, plus a helpline.

Book an appointment with a doctor for your child so you can start the clock to ask for a referral to a specialist toileting service.

My plan for managing toileting difficulties:

'E': What emotions do I expect I will be feeling?

'A': What actions can I use that will best soothe me?

'S': How can I stop with compassion, to support my child and I through this?

'E': How am I hoping to feel by the end?

My child is sooo fussy at mealtimes

In our clinic, we hear themes that come up time and time again for parents about their children's eating. For example:

- Children disliking the taste of anything green (especially vegetables; Brussels sprouts often get a special mention)

- Mushrooms are eyed with suspicion

- A strong dislike for fish . . . although breaded fish is more readily accepted

- Raw tomatoes are considered to be inedible (unless turned into ketchup or as part of a pizza topping)

However, some parents have children who seem to be more fussy than the average child.

The difficult issue with feeding children is that it is one of the basic parenting tasks that we are all programmed to do, right from the very first day our children are born. And, while some children seem to be natural 'foodies' from the start and love to eat everything on their plate (and on their parents' plates!), other children find it much harder to try unfamiliar foods and can be vocal about not eating them.

An added difficulty with feeding issues is that we are aware as adults of how important it is to feed our children enough food each day, while also giving them a wide range of different foods. In fact, we receive messages day-in, day-out about the importance of good nutrition for our children, whether this is to:

- Prevent childhood obesity – which has been a government target for many years

- Ensure our children have the correct vitamins and minerals to be healthy

- Prevent our children from the risk of health conditions linked to nutrition, such as childhood diabetes and teeth decay

- Teach our children good eating habits, for them to continue with into adulthood

- Ensure our children have sufficient energy from their food to manage the school day, extracurricular clubs, etc.

- Stop our children from having 'sugar highs' (this is often mentioned by parents during children's birthday parties, when children consume significantly more sugary drinks and snacks than normal), and so on

Thus, there is significant pressure to make sure that we give our children enough of the 'right' sorts of foods, and not too many of the 'wrong' sorts of foods, but this may be easier said than done.

Some children simply find it harder than others to try unfamiliar foods, or to eat a variety of different foods, and this can be for a whole host of reasons.

Genetics

We know that some conditions can increase the likelihood of children finding it difficult to eat a wide variety of foods. For example, many autistic children eat only a limited range, which can be due to them having a categorisation issue. This means that if a food is slightly different to what they usually eat, it isn't considered to be from the same category and, therefore, it's considered unsafe to eat. For example, supermarket own-brand oven chips may be rejected, as the child does not see them as being 'true' chips, given the subtle differences between them and their usual and accepted branded oven chips. Or batter that has slightly overbrowned in the oven may not be considered edible, as the child expects batter to be a golden-brown colour. Many autistic children also try to keep their routines and environment the same, to manage their stress and anxiety levels. Part of this includes trying to keep their diet the same, with identical foods or meals each day. In addition, it is fairly common for autistic young people to have overactive sensory systems, which can affect how they react to the foods they eat, as they struggle with the sensory aspect of the food – such as its taste, its texture, its smell, etc.

It is worth adding that a number of children who are not autistic also have an inborn genetic hypersensitivity to food. And, if you think about eating, it is easy to understand what a sensory experience it is:

<u>Taste:</u> This is the most obvious sense triggered during eating and some children struggle with certain tastes or find them too overwhelming to cope with. The average baby is born with around ten thousand taste buds, but over time these gradually shrink and reduce in number. Children will, therefore, experience tastes much more strongly than their grandparents do. Just to complicate things further, around 25% of us are 'supertasters' and are, therefore, much more sensitive to tastes than around 45–50% of 'average' tasters, and 25% of 'non-tasters'. Being a supertaster may contribute towards food fussiness, as a child can struggle to enjoy the tastes they are experiencing if they find the flavours too intense.

<u>Texture:</u> Foods all have different textures. Think about how a prawn cracker dissolves in your mouth, compared to a banana that has a squishy, soft texture. And think about a roast potato with its crunchy outside but soft middle compared to a mushroom that can be slimy when you chew it. Some children love this range of textures, but others struggle and find certain textures unpleasant in their mouths.

<u>Smell:</u> Foods can have pretty strong smells, too. Imagine the smell of an onion frying, or bacon sizzling in a pan. The smell of foods can put children off eating them.

<u>Sound:</u> Sounds can play a role as well, as children can tune in to the noise their food makes – such as the crunching of carrots or apples. Sounds of other people eating may also be difficult and put children off sitting at a dinner table and eating alongside others.

Often, when we see children with selective eating in the clinic, their parents remember that they were also picky eaters when they were children. Therefore, it may be that selective eating is within a family's genetics, so it gets passed down from parent to child.

A final genetic difficulty that some children must deal with is having an allergy. It is completely understandable for children who have an allergy (or allergies) to feel cautious about eating new foods, particularly if they have had a scary experience with an allergic reaction during a mealtime. Their fear is protective, as it will act to prevent the child from having another allergy response. However, it is not always helpful if you have worked out that the new food is safe for them, but the child is still too hesitant to try it.

Learning

Mealtimes are naturally social experiences. If you think back to weaning your child, you have been present throughout most (if not all) of your child's mealtimes to feed them and check if it is safe for them to chew and swallow the new foods. As your child has grown older, you have continued to be a presence during mealtimes – cooking and serving up meals, maybe eating alongside them, and responding to your child as they ate, or didn't eat the foods you gave them.

All of the mealtime interactions you have had with your child may well have shaped the eaters they then become. Take this example:

Example

Sarah was happy to admit to being a naturally anxious parent and she found mealtimes particularly stressful given her early years with her five-year-old son, Joseph. Joseph had suffered from a tongue tie as a baby and so found it hard to take her milk, which resulted in him losing weight during his first two weeks of life. Joseph had an operation to resolve his tongue tie, and Sarah also switched to formula milk, but she continued to feel highly anxious that Joseph was not having sufficient milk for his needs and might not regain the lost weight. When she started to wean Joseph, he seemed to particularly enjoy shop-bought, smooth purees and did not accept the homemade purees she made him as readily. So, Sarah decided to stick with the pre-prepared purees he enjoyed.

However, as Joseph got older, Sarah felt pressure to increase the range of purees she gave him, to include purees with more lumps that required chewing. Yet, when Sarah gave these to Joseph, she felt anxious that he was not eating as much as she expected and so she always finished a meal by giving him a sachet of his preferred smooth-style puree. Over time, Joseph ate less and less of the lumpy purees and would instead wait for the smooth ones, as he had learnt that they would be offered to him if he didn't eat much of the lumpier purees. Eventually, Joseph stopped eating any of the lumpy meals at all.

Sarah was understandably worried about this and tempted Joseph to eat any finger foods he might accept, to try to progress his eating. She was able to get Joseph to accept smooth yoghurts with no lumps in them and was also happy when he ate some soft white bread, and when he tried a few sweets. However, when Sarah tried to get Joseph to eat any dinners, he refused and waited the meal out, knowing that he would eventually be offered some milk, a smooth puree, sweets or bread.

Sarah recognised that Joseph's diet was limited and felt very anxious about this. So she kept offering him any solid food she could think of, and over time Joseph started to eat a variety of biscuits and chocolate bars, which she kept giving him to ensure he consumed enough calories each day. However, Joseph continued to refuse the healthier meals that his mum gave him, knowing that he would eventually be offered an alternative that he liked better and which was less challenging for him.

You can see in the example that, over time, Joseph developed the protective strategy of avoiding one type of food (lumpy or less palatable food), as he had learnt that if he waited long enough he would eventually be given a familiar food type that he liked. However, this had the unintended consequence of Joseph not getting used to lumpier textures and having a very limited diet.

Children can also learn to fear trying new foods if they have experienced a significant and scary allergy response to something they have eaten. Other children may change their eating habits if they have been unwell or are admitted to hospital, particularly if they have been unable to eat normally due to their illness or condition. They may even learn to associate particular foods with unpleasant symptoms (such as feeling or being sick).

Spend a few minutes filling in Worksheet 36, to note the relevant factors that you think have contributed to your child's fussy eating:

Worksheet 36: Reasons why my child eats a limited number of foods

Genetic reasons

(e.g. a condition like autism, sensory processing needs, family patterns of being a selective eater, allergy, etc.)

Learning reasons

(e.g. a difficult experience with eating, your own parental reactions to your child's eating, etc.)

Let's go back to the EASE model we have used throughout this book. It is understandable that fussy eating can cause strong **'E' emotions**, such as:

Anxiety: fearing your child will lose weight and that they might not have enough energy for the day or they could become ill because of eating the 'wrong' foods.

Guilt: being aware that children 'should' be able to eat many types of foods and feeling it's your fault that they don't.

Failure: your child's problems with eating and mealtimes may feel like a failure of parenting.

Sadness: that your child can't enjoy a normal eating experience, or that your family can't go out for meals or to restaurants like other families can.

Embarrassment: when other adults find out about your child's selective eating.

Anger: may occur if you've spent time preparing food and your child then rejects it. Anger can also be linked to the difficult situation you and your child are in.

Disgust: about the foods your child chooses.

Despair: that your child will never eat a wide range of foods.

What emotions are you feeling about your child's selective eating? Is it just one, or multiple emotions? Do these emotions affect your thoughts about mealtimes, the memories that enter your mind about past meals with your child, and how relaxed or not your body feels as you approach feeding times? Complete Worksheet 37:

Worksheet 37: My emotions

Our emotional response often affects our reactions. For example, if we are feeling anxious about our child not eating enough, we might be more likely to take a gentle approach to mealtimes and offer alternatives that we know our child will eat. Whereas, if we're feeling angry with our child for leaving a meal, we may be more likely to shout and refuse to give them any other food.

How do your emotions affect your next steps as a parent? Complete Worksheet 38:

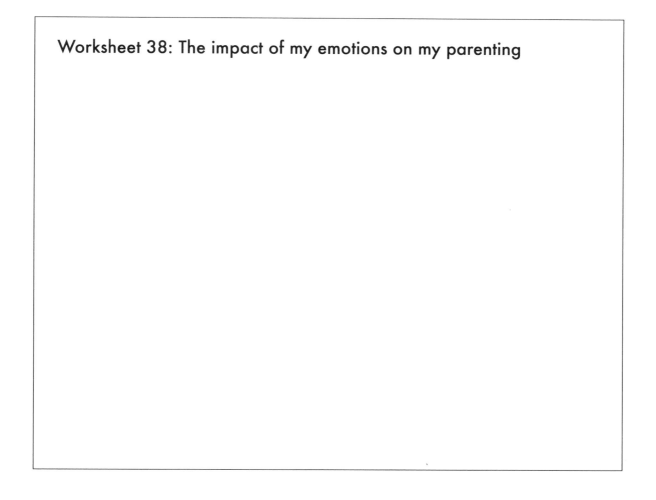

Worksheet 38: The impact of my emotions on my parenting

As we can see from Worksheet 38, our emotions can make it harder for us to manage our children's restricted eating. Therefore, it is important to undertake the next step of the EASE model: **actions to soothe,** in order to manage these difficult emotions, so we are in the best place possible to manage a difficult mealtime moment.

Look back at Chapter 3 page 58 to remind yourself of the most helpful steps you can take to regain control over your difficult emotions. Do you need to make any adjustments to your actions to soothe to help them work with a mealtime? For example, you might not be able to take five minutes to calm down if you are on the point of serving food and it would otherwise go cold. But you could take one minute to tell yourself a few helpful 'cheerleading statements' while you're away from the meal.

In order to help your child feel ready to try more types of foods, you need to implement some **stopping with compassion** strategies: both for yourself, so you are able to help your child eat more foods, and for your child to feel sufficiently ready to do so, too.

Compassionate strategies for yourself as a parent

Look back at Worksheet 37 on page 194, where you listed your emotions when your child is selective in their eating. Each emotion will alter how your critical mind talks to you in that mealtime moment. See the box below for some examples:

Examples of how emotions change what your critical mind says to you

Anxiety:

'My child is going to end up poorly and I couldn't cope with that'

'What if they don't eat anything today? I'll never manage it and then they'll be up all night hungry'

Guilt:

'I'm such a dreadful parent'

'It's all my fault'

'No one is as bad as me with meals'

Failure:

'I can't do this'

'I'm hopeless at it'

'I'm such an idiot to have caused these problems'

Sadness:

'It's all completely hopeless'

'I will never have a nice mealtime with my child'

Embarrassment:

'Everyone is looking at me and judging me'

'They can see that I'm bad at this'

Anger:

'I spent ages on this meal and for what point?'

'I'm such a loser as a parent'

Your critical mind can feed off such negative emotions. Therefore, it is really important to touch base with the wisdom of your compassionate mind, to help you think in a healthier way about your role *now* with your child's eating. This will take great courage and strength, as the critical mind can be very strong at such moments.

Look back at Exercise 1 on page 65 and use this template to work through what your compassionate mind would tell you about your parenting, supporting your child's restricted eating. Jot it down in Worksheet 39:

Worksheet 39: My compassionate mind about my parenting

(For example, 'This is tough, but you're doing the best you can.' 'You know your child has always found eating this food difficult, so it's OK for progress to be slow. The key thing is that you're moving forwards.' 'Everyone who loves you knows that you're trying hard with their eating and won't be judging you.')

Remember to connect with compassion in your body, too, such as by keeping a neutral facial expression, a more open posture and a calm and kind voice tone, as this makes such a big difference.

Compassionate strategies to try with your child

Keep your child out of a threat state

Unfortunately, it can be easy for your child to shift into a threat state when they are being encouraged or told to eat different foods, particularly if they are fearful of doing so. This makes them much less likely to risk eating something unfamiliar to them. Therefore, the first key point is to aim for a relaxed attitude around mealtimes, not putting pressure on your child to try anything new but being ready to praise them if they do. This can be easier said than done, which is why it is important to use your compassionate mind on yourself first, to help you remain calm.

Remember: Strike while the iron is cold

Usually, the best time to introduce new foods is when your child is in a calm, relaxed state, rather than overly tired or stressed from a busy day.

Use child-friendly language about new foods

It's all in the marketing!

It's amazing how much our language can make a difference, to tempt children into being curious about unfamiliar foods. For younger children, it can be helpful to use enticing language, such as adapting the names of new foods to suit their interests. For example:

Green vegetable pasta sauce/pesto	Incredible Hulk sauce
Different fruit	Eating the rainbow
Carrots or potatoes	Minecraft carrots and Minecraft potatoes
Spaghetti	Mario spaghetti

Older children may be more aware of food groups and nutrition, which are usually taught to them at school. If your child appears to be interested in this area, feel free to chat to them in a relaxed way about the benefits of certain foods from a nutritional perspective. For example, describing a piece of chicken as being full of protein, which will help them to grow taller. Or telling them about how milk is packed with calcium and it will make their bones get stronger. We've worked with some teenagers who are keen to research for themselves the nutrient content of foods, so they can take control over which new foods to try.

Keep it fun

Adapt mealtimes so they are fun or playful, to keep your child in a soothed state. For example, put out buffets that include food they will and won't eat to help them get used to seeing their less preferred foods (and perhaps trying them). Have a mini party with new foods presented in exciting ways (e.g. using a Halloween theme to present foods differently). Or you could provide meals that can be eaten with hands rather than cutlery (e.g. naan or chapattis with a curry, prawn crackers with a stir fry, tortilla wraps with a Mexican, etc.). You can even invent 'silly' rules to increase the fun of a mealtime, such as everyone eating a meal with just a spoon or trying to eat with the 'wrong' hand (e.g. their left hand if they are right-handed). Or making pictures with the food on their plates. Remember to stay relaxed throughout these fun meals rather than slipping into the tendency to prompt or insist that your child tries some of the new foods. Being around the new foods may be a good first step, even if your child doesn't try them to begin with.

Expose them to food outside mealtimes

It can be helpful to expose your child to different foods outside mealtimes. For example:

- asking for their help with cooking (even if it's for something they can't eat, as yet)

- using food for art and craft activities (e.g. making pictures, jewellery or towers with different shapes of pasta, or making a bird feeder with cereal)

- getting them to help unpack a food shop into the cupboards and fridge

- having fruit and vegetables freely available and in sight at all times and giving your child permission to help themselves to these whenever they fancy

Ask for help from an older child

Humans are social animals and we naturally make comparisons between ourselves and the people around us, particularly those whom we perceive as being 'higher in the pecking order' than we are. We can use this fact to our advantage with eating difficulties. If you know an older child who is a good eater, whom your child looks up to (e.g. an older cousin or family friend), it can be helpful to have them over for a meal. The key here is to remain relaxed and *not* make any comments about what they eat compared to your child. You just need to provide food that your child will eat, plus unacceptable foods, too (that the older child enjoys), and let your child watch what happens.

A step-by-step plan

Biology tells us that we generally need repeated exposure to foods before our taste systems know whether we like them or not. Therefore, you can develop a plan with your child to gradually introduce new foods for them to eat. This is most powerful if your child is in control of what food is picked. They might even shift into a drive system to research possible options or go shopping with you to choose what foods to try. At the start, these new foods might need to be a food close to one they already consume, to help them stay out of a threat. For example, if they eat a specific brand of salted crisps, they may want to try a supermarket own-brand of salted crisps. Or if they eat fries, you might try crispy potato wedges. The aim with these early foods is to help your child feel greater confidence with eating a more varied diet, rather than being overly focused on the types of new foods they are eating.

For children who are particularly anxious about unfamiliar foods, it may be too much for them to move straight in to eating a new item. Instead, you may need to use your compassionate wisdom and try a gentler approach to new foods, such as your child tolerating a new food on their plate for a few days; then smelling the food; next, they might rub it on their lips; and a day later, perhaps put it on their tongue (and then spit it out) before working up to swallowing it.

You can encourage your child to rate each new food for 'yumminess', where 1 = really disgusting and 10 = incredibly yummy. They can then track if the yumminess number changes the more times they try it.

Once your child has tried one new food on a few occasions, you can then look at their plan and agree on the next food they will try, and so on.

Rewards!

Alongside your praise and warm, relaxed approach, it can be really useful to use rewards for when your child tries a new food, both to motivate them into changing their eating patterns and also to demonstrate to them how proud you are of their bravery to eat an unfamiliar food. Look back at Chapter 5, page 135, for a reminder about rewards for your child.

You will be familiar with the last step in the EASE model by now, looking at your 'E' emotions to check how you are feeling now about your child's eating. It is worth noting that selective eating can take a long time to change in children, so you may notice that your emotions do not shift as quickly as you would like. However, look for the signs of progress or change. You may also spot times when your difficult emotions are triggered once more during mealtimes. If this is the case, see these as 'learning opportunities' to fine-tune the strategies you are using and, if your child is old enough, chat to them about how you can 'tweak' the plan, to keep them moving forwards.

Next steps

If your child is under five years old and is still struggling to eat a range of foods after trying these ideas, contact your health visitor. You can also talk to your doctor about your concerns about your child's eating or seek support from a dietician.

My plan for managing my child's restricted eating

'E': What emotions do I expect I will be feeling?

'A': What actions can I use that will best soothe me?

'S': How can I stop with compassion, to support my child and me through this?

'E': How am I hoping I will feel by the end?

(I can also note down any learning I make here)

My child is anxious whenever we have to separate

Separation anxiety can be distressing for both children and their parents. However, for babies and young children, it is a sign that they are attached to their parent. It means that your child has formed a strong bond with you and this is incredibly important in their emotional and social development. For many children, they will have phases when they become more clingy and this can become more pronounced around times of change, when they feel unsafe, are insecure or are hungry, tired or overwhelmed.

Separation anxiety and fear of strangers is normal in young children between the ages of six months and three years and it is considered to be a typical part of your child's development.

For some children, separation anxiety can continue into later childhood and start to have an impact on their lives and the lives of their parents. For example, it can mean children do not want to be left alone at bedtime, cannot go to friends' houses or parties without you and may become very distressed when they are left at school. This can cause lots of worries for parents and is understandably very difficult for all involved. It can affect a parent's ability to go out in the day or evening, be on time for work or even to attend work.

Understandably, many emotions and thoughts are triggered for parents when their child starts to show separation anxiety. The first step, '**E**', is to spot the **emotions** in yourself that are triggered by your child's separation anxiety.

Here are some examples of the common emotions and thoughts that parents experience:

- Anxiety: 'They're so distressed.' 'I can't leave them.' 'How am I going to work?' 'What am I going to do about that party next week?' 'It doesn't feel safe.'

- Frustration: 'Why can't they separate?' 'They don't behave like this when their dad drops them off.'

- Anger: 'I have to work!' 'This is ridiculous.' 'It's always me!'

- Hopelessness: 'I am never going to be able to leave her.'

- Embarrassment: 'All the other children are able to be left at the party.' 'Why is it always her?'

- Guilt: 'Have I done something to cause this?' 'Maybe my anxiety has rubbed off on her.'

It can be difficult to consider how to manage separation anxiety, as it invariably brings up so many complex emotions for parents. It takes real bravery to recognise these emotions in yourself and what may be coming up for you as your child faces separation. By recognising our emotions, we can then consider ways to soothe ourselves, in order to move forward with taking a compassionate parenting approach to manage the child's separation anxiety. Please note down any emotions and thoughts you may experience regarding your own child's separation anxiety in Worksheet 40:

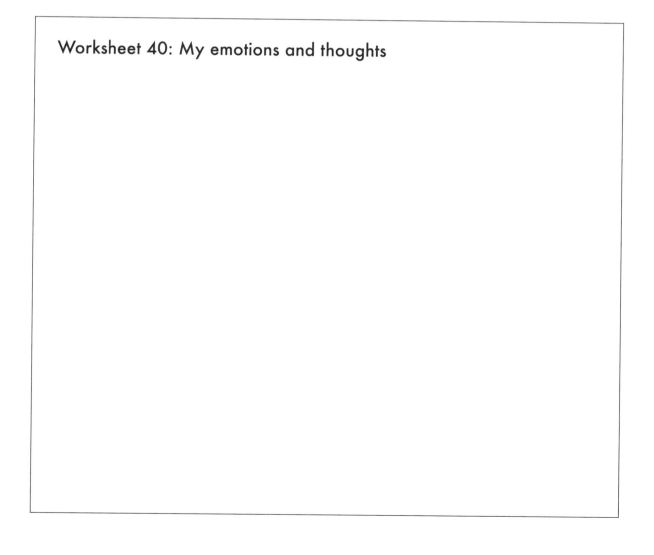

Worksheet 40: My emotions and thoughts

After spotting which emotions are present, it is helpful to undertake step two of EASE:

'A', taking an **action to soothe** yourself before you start to consider how to support your child with separation anxiety. This will help you achieve the right mindset to tackle this struggle for your child whenever it flares up. Take a few deep breaths or take another soothing action that you identified in the 'Actions to Soothe' section on page 57. If you have time, try practising a soothing breathing rhythm for five minutes.

We can now move on to the **'S'** of **stopping with compassion.**

It is important to recognise the reasons why your child may be experiencing separation anxiety. You may also have your own worries and hesitancies about leaving your child, so it is important to consider these with compassion, as it will help you to move forward with your compassionate parenting plan.

Let's look back to the iceberg example from Chapter 4 on page 73.

Try connecting with the reasons your child is struggling with separation anxiety. Here are some suggestions:

Things to consider	Compassionate perspective
Is it a normal phase? Remember that between the ages of six months to three years, separation anxiety is a normal phase of development	Try to reassure yourself that this is a phase. It is understandable you may feel worried about it, as this is hard for you and your child. Consider the strong, wise version of yourself and how they may support your child during this phase of their life
Is the environment right?	Some children struggle to separate when the environment they are being asked to separate into does not meet their needs. Take a few moments to consider your child's temperament. Now consider the environment your child is going into. Are they suited? Does the environment need to be modified to suit the child's needs? This can sometimes be the case for young people who are autistic, given their sensory, social and emotional needs

Are they ready developmentally?	Many parents are keen to encourage their children to have sleepovers or playdates without them or to go away on residential trips. Other parents may be more cautious and may host playdates, but not do sleepovers. Every child is different. Some may be really keen to go away and others may find it hard. Consider your own ideas around this and whether they match the needs of your child. Are they ready for this step or do they need more time? Is this really in their best interest at this stage? Is there another way to help them to separate?
Worries about what they are doing when they're there	For many school-age children, their fears of separation often stem from worries about what happens when they separate. For example, we have worked with children who feel unable to use or ask to use the toilet at school or are unable to ask an adult for help. They may worry that their caregiver will not pick them up or be late. It is important to consider your own fears or behaviours when you try to encourage your child to separate. We parents bring our own fears and worries with us on the journey. This is not our fault and is part of being human. It takes strength and courage to recognise this and to use wisdom to consider how best to move forward

Parenting ideas to try

1.   Support them through the developmental phase

For babies and toddlers, it is normal to experience separation anxiety. They often need a lot of love and comfort to support them through this phase. If the separation is not necessary, then it may be helpful to reduce the amount of separation time and to practise short separations from your baby or toddler to begin with. This will reassure them that you are going to return. Leaving them with someone they know and are very comfortable with can help. If the separation is necessary (e.g. nursery), try to find another safe, trusted person at this place, whom your child feels is able to provide them with nurture and comfort. If the child is not connecting with their key worker, then it may be helpful to explore whether another key worker would be better. The connection between adult and child is fundamental. It may be helpful for your child to take a transitional object with them to nursery and for you to talk to the key worker about how you soothe your child, so they can soothe the same way you do.

2.   Talk to your child about their fears and worries regarding separation

Even very young children benefit from a space to talk about how they are feeling. One child we worked with could vocalise their distress at going to nursery before the age of two by saying, 'nooo school'. They may not be able to tell you why at this age but helping them to put their feelings into words can be helpful. For children with more complex language, it can be helpful to set aside the time to listen so that you understand what their worries are. For example, they may worry that you won't be there to pick them up, or that you will be late, or that someone won't be able to take them to the toilet if they need it. Reassure your child that they have been very brave in talking about these worries and that many other people feel this way, too.

3.   Address the worries and make a plan

It is important to start addressing your child's worries about the place they are separating to by making a plan with them that supports your child. This plan can then be shared and updated with your child so they feel safe and supported. For example, it may be helpful for your child to have dedicated toilet breaks in a quiet toilet or have a key person who provides regular check-ins with them, or a plan around what happens if a parent is late to pick them up. If your child gets overwhelmed from being with too many new people, or by being in a busy environment, agree upon a place they can go to 'decompress' for a short period with a key person from this setting. Or let your child bring along a book or game that they can turn to if they need time out from everything. For some children, it may be that the environment is not suited to their needs. Sometimes a change of setting can make a marked difference to separating.

4.   Your response

As we have discussed, separation anxiety can be very emotive for parents. It is important for you to recognise these feelings and to note how you may be displaying them around the time of separation. It is not your fault you feel like this. It is completely natural. Recognising your initial responses can support you to then consider whether there is a better response for your child. For example, do they need to see a calm, confident body posture from you to reassure them everything is OK? It may be helpful to practise some of the exercises noted in our previous chapters about stepping into this calm, confident role. Warming up using your soothing activities is very important.

5.   Build up a gradual ladder of ways you can start separating from your child for short periods of time

If separation anxiety is getting in the way of your child's life and ability to access things they enjoy, it can be helpful to gradually begin to expose your child to separating in a way that they feel in control of. You could get a big bit of paper and lots of small Post-it notes. Ask your child to write lots of different options for separation (e.g. going to a playdate without Mummy/Daddy; sleeping over at grandparents), including some very small steps (e.g. Mummy/Daddy going into another room when Grandma is visiting; Mummy/Daddy going into the garden for two minutes when you're watching TV). Then ask your child to put them in order of how difficult they are. You could also allocate prizes for each step. It is important that your child is in control of choosing when these steps are taken. If they feel out of control or pushed, it could set things back.

The last step of EASE is to look at your '**E' emotions now**, to see how you have got on with creating a plan to manage separation anxiety. You can ask yourself:

- Has there been a change in the emotions that were initially triggered?

- Do I need to take any more 'A' actions to soothe strategies to help myself with these emotions?

- Have I been able to consider my own feelings and my child's struggles within a compassionate framework?

- Is there anything else I may need to do to support me with this process?

Next steps

If your child continues to struggle with separation anxiety (and they are of school age), you may need to seek further support from a suitably qualified professional. This is something you can talk to your doctor about.

'My child takes their anger out on me'

It's a universal fact that we all feel angry at times and have occasions when we don't control our own anger as well as we know we should. This is because anger is a normal emotion for humans and, as we outlined in Chapter 1, it had evolutionary advantages (such as allowing our Stone Age ancestors to protect their group from attack by other groups).

We can see the presence of anger in infancy – for example, some babies 'shout cry' at their parents for not feeding them quickly enough when they are hungry for milk. And everyone expects toddlers to have tantrums, as they have not yet learnt to control their strong desires and impulses. Over the course of childhood and adolescence, we hope that our children gain increasing control over their anger, but this is not always easy for them, because of genetic and learning factors.

Genetic factors

We all have different personalities and this means that some of us naturally have shorter fuses than others. This is also true for children. Some youngsters seem to be born with a laid-back, chilled attitude, whereas others are more feisty, and can shift into anger more quickly. If this has been passed down in your children's genes, it may be that other family members also share a feisty side. In fact, it's fairly common for at least one of the parents we see in clinic whose child has anger issues to remember having had a short temper themselves when they were younger (and they sometimes still have a short fuse as adults).

Alongside personality influences, some neurodevelopmental conditions can influence anger. For example, children with ADHD may be more at risk of acting in an angry way, as their impulsivity means that it is harder for them to resist responding with strong, angry emotions, and they may end up doing so before they have had a chance to think.

Hormones play a significant role in emotional regulation during adolescence. During puberty, testosterone can increase ten- to twentyfold in boys, with some showing higher levels of this hormone than others. And a link has been established between teenage boys with higher testosterone levels and more impatient and impulsive behaviour. The fluctuations of oestrogen and progesterone in teenage girls can also contribute to angry outbursts and some girls struggle with hormonal imbalances, which can intensify such symptoms.

We also all have some emotions that we slip into more easily than others and, for some people, their 'default' feeling is anger, as outlined in the table below:

Child's true emotion	How the child could show this true emotion	How the child actually shows their emotion through anger
Fear about running a race at sports day	Becoming tearful and hyperventilating on the morning of sports day and expressing feeling scared about the race	Starting to shout at their teacher that they're 'not going to do the stupid race'
Sadness about doing badly in a test	Crying when getting the test result and being withdrawn for the rest of the day	Yelling at their parents when they get home, throwing their belongings around their bedroom and refusing to discuss the test

Unfortunately, responding in anger rather than with the true emotion generally results in a child being misunderstood and their needs not being met. If we take the example of shouting at a teacher about a sports day race, there is every chance that the teacher will give the child a consequence for the angry outburst and the child will still be expected to run the race, with no nurturing or compassion. Whereas, if the child was able to show their true fear about the race, they are much more likely to receive the caring support they need.

Learning factors

As we have explored throughout this book, our behaviour is shaped by the responses and the messages we receive. Let's take an example related to our child's anger to highlight this:

Example

Zuri spotted a lollipop she really fancied in the supermarket and asked her mum if she would buy it for her. Zuri's mum was busy at the checkout and hurriedly replied that she'd bought plenty of food at the supermarket. Zuri could have one of these items when she got home.

Zuri was not happy with this answer and lost her temper. She shouted at her mum as they stood in the checkout queue, 'I WANT the lollipop, Mum! It's NOT FAIR! You're such a MEAN mum, and everyone knows it!'

Zuri's mum was naturally embarrassed by her daughter's outburst and hated that the other shoppers turned around to look at her. So, she quietly picked up the lollipop from the shelf, showed it to Zuri and added it to her shopping. Zuri instantly calmed down and was pleased when her mum paid for the lollipop quickly, so she could suck on it while her mum finished bagging up the shopping.

As we can see from this example, Zuri's angry response resulted in her gaining the lollipop she so greatly wanted. Unfortunately, this interaction also taught Zuri that if she showed her mum anger (particularly when out in public), her mum was more likely to give in to her and give Zuri what she wanted. The next time Zuri and her mum were out in public and Zuri spotted a treat or toy that she liked the look of, but her mum said 'no', what do you think Zuri did next . . .?

Yes, that's right, she showed her angry response again, in the hope that it would be as effective as the last time.

Complete Worksheet 41 to identify the factors you think contribute to your child's struggles with anger:

Worksheet 41: Factors contributing to my child's struggle with anger

Genetic factors

(e.g. personality, neurodevelopmental or other difficulties, hormones, anger being their go-to emotion, etc.)

Learning factors

(e.g. interactions with parents and others)

It can be useful to work through the 'formulation of my child' from page 99 to understand the reasons your child has adopted the protective strategy of turning to anger. You could also consider the unintended consequences (such as them being told off and getting into trouble), plus how your child's critical mind may be contributing to their anger. This formulation will also help you in the next steps of EASE.

The EASE model for anger

Compassionate parenting can help us deal effectively with our children's anger whenever it may strike (including when out in public!)

'E' for emotion

It is important to be honest with yourself about which of your emotions are triggered when your child shows an angry response. This is because we can become overwhelmed by our own emotions when we see our child become angry. This effects your ability to parent in the way you've planned as it can cloud and change your intentions, thoughts and bodily sensations (e.g. you may become tense and hot, with a faster heart rate). Therefore, while you may have the best intentions to implement a parenting strategy, it could be impossible to do so in the moment, because you are overwhelmed by your own emotional state.

Common emotions we see in parents whose children are angry include:

Anger	It is not unusual to feel angry when someone else is being angry with us. For example, if you were involved in a minor car accident and the other driver started shouting that you had caused the accident, it would not be unusual for you to shout back about how it was, in fact, their driving that had caused the issue
	This angry response in the face of another person's anger makes evolutionary sense, given that our Stone Age ancestors needed to quickly retaliate in an angry and aggressive way if they were in danger from another group or a powerful predator
	The same pattern is true for us, as parents, and for our children. If they speak to us in an angry tone, it is not unusual for us to shift into an angry mode as well
Shame	Despite anger being a normal human emotion, there is a great deal of stigma associated with it, which leads many people to have a shame reaction when their children demonstrate anger. Shame can occur in public when one feels at risk of being judged by other people, or when reflecting on the parent you wish to be, or the child you wish to have, and knowing that their angry responses do not fit with this ideal picture

Embarrassment	Embarrassment is common for parents – especially when their children demonstrate anger in a public setting
Anxiety	Parents can also feel anxiety about their children's angry and aggressive actions. We often fear that our children will continue to show similar anger as they age and end up in serious fights, get into trouble with the law, be expelled from their school, or be unable to make close relationships in future. Parents may also fear that other family members could get hurt by their children when aggression is around
Sadness	This sadness is associated with not being able to have the relationship you wish to have with your child, due to their anger; or sadness about them getting into trouble for their angry actions. Parents may also feel sad about being unable to go on family outings or share family experiences, in case their child becomes angry in that setting
Guilt	Guilt is often present and may centre on the fact that your child is struggling with anger and you haven't managed to change this issue

From our clinical experience, it is rare for parents to experience just one of these emotions. Instead, we find that parents tend to experience multiple emotions during a child's angry outburst, and all of these can have an impact on how they then respond, as you can see in the example:

Example

Arman was in the living room at home and wanted to watch his favourite YouTuber on the family TV. However, his younger sister, Soraya, had beaten him to it and was already watching her preferred YouTuber. Arman tried to grab the remote control from Soraya to change the channel, but she was quick to move it under her sofa cushion. He then punched Soraya in the arm and shouted at her to give him the remote control.

A parent feeling predominately anger would be likely to shout at Arman for punching Soraya, might call him negative labels (e.g. 'You're such a horrible child!') and give him a much bigger consequence than they would otherwise if they had remained calm.

A parent feeling mostly anxiety might plead with Arman to be kinder to his sister and repeat how he can't keep acting this way, or he'll be in big trouble in the future.

A parent in a sad state may start to cry after witnessing this situation and tell both children about how everything is wrong with their family and that things will never get better if they keep acting this way.

Which emotions do you tend to feel when your child is demonstrating anger? Complete Worksheet 42:

Worksheet 42: My emotions:

As you can see, our emotions greatly affect our ability to parent children who are showing anger. Therefore, it is incredibly important to undertake the next step of the EASE model, so you are ready to put compassionate parenting in place.

'A' actions to soothe

Before starting the compassionate parenting strategies, follow one of the actions that helps you regulate your emotions once more, from the worksheet you filled in on page 31. You may choose to use an action to soothe that takes a longer time to complete (such as making yourself a cup of tea or ringing a friend for support), if you feel your child would benefit from having some space away from you (or you need space from your child). Or you may need to choose a faster action to soothe (e.g. a cheerleading statement), if you need to stay in a difficult situation and act fast. Referring back to your completed 'formulation of my child' (from page 99) may also beneficial, as it can be much easier to remain regulated with your own emotions, if you understand the reasons behind your child's anger – rather than just seeing the behaviour as 'bad' or 'naughty'. Plus, try to see the situation through your child's eyes, at their age, rather than yours, as an adult.

Note down the best actions to soothe that you can try in Worksheet 43, when your child is angry:

Worksheet 43: Actions to soothe when my child is angry:

Hopefully, you feel in a better position to manage your child's anger at this point and can move on to the next step in compassionate parenting.

Stopping with compassion

We can now move on to the **'S'** of **stopping with compassion**.

When formulating and sharing a plan to support your child to manage their anger, it is important to strike while the iron is cold.

As mentioned in Chapter 4, it is important to first consider the iceberg analogy. The behaviour (e.g. hitting, swearing, slamming doors) is the tip of the iceberg. We want to consider what is beneath the surface.

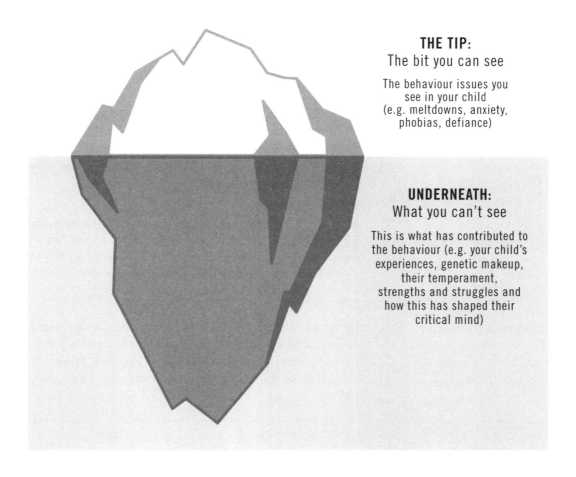

THE TIP:
The bit you can see

The behaviour issues you
see in your child
(e.g. meltdowns, anxiety,
phobias, defiance)

UNDERNEATH:
What you can't see

This is what has contributed to
the behaviour (e.g. your child's
experiences, genetic makeup,
their temperament,
strengths and struggles and
how this has shaped their
critical mind)

Spend some time thinking about what may be causing your child to behave in the way they are. Once you have done this, you can consider whether the following strategies will be helpful. As we have already mentioned, there is no one model or approach that will manage all these struggles, which is why you will need to consider the strategies carefully and then decide if they will be helpful for your child and, if so, how you apply them compassionately.

Here are some ideas to try:

Spot and address the triggers (underneath the iceberg)	Angry outbursts often occur from the same triggers. For example, when your child is in a busy and overwhelming setting, if they are hungry, if they've not had sufficient exercise, if they are overtired from their day, or have generally not had enough sleep (Dawes et al. 2018). Therefore, it can be worth using your wisdom to spot such patterns and make a compassionate plan around them, as your child is likely to need kindness and support to cope with any triggers. For example, giving them a snack straight after school, while you remain quiet on the walk or drive home until they have 'decompressed' from school. Otherwise, they may end up shifting into anger or having an outburst
	For some children, their brains have simply not matured enough to cope with their triggers. For example, some children really struggle with losing or with sharing. In these cases, it may be helpful to try to reduce their exposure to such triggers while they learn the necessary skills or until their brain is more mature
Household boundaries	Re-establishing the household boundaries and rules together can be very helpful. You can sit down together as a family and draw up these rules. Try to make them what you *want* to see rather than what you don't want to see, e.g. 'kind bodies' rather than 'no hitting'
Logical and natural consequences	Tied into this discussion may be the question of what happens if someone breaks the household rules. You can involve your child/children in these discussions. For example, if someone swears and the household rule states that the person has to put some money in a 'swear jar'. Or, when they are calm, they may need to apologise to the people involved
	It is important that these rules are discussed when everyone is calm and not when your child is angry, as this is likely to escalate the situation further
Creating a calm space	If your child is struggling to manage their big emotions, wisdom tells us that they need help with learning the difficult skill of shifting into their soothing drive, in order to calm down. Get your

	child involved in creating a space that feels safe and has things they can use to calm down. Practising these strategies when they are calm is essential. For example, in this space do they have a big pillow they can squeeze or some fidget toys? Doing this together can mean that you can have time to discuss why it is important to have space when we are cross
Make a plan for outbursts	It can be helpful to talk to your child about a plan for when feelings become too much. For example, what will you do and try not to do; what you would like them to do and not to do, and why The zones of regulation can be a useful tool to support these discussions. There is a reference for the zones of regulation at the end of the book, if you'd like to learn more about this approach
Learning the art of de-escalation	As we discussed in Chapter 3, it is important to consider your own reaction and how you will respond when your child is cross. Go back to the sat nav analogy in Chapter 5 and consider how you might react in situations where your child has lost control
Supporting your child with the underlying struggle	As we mentioned earlier, it is important to consider which skills your child may need to build up so they can better manage their emotions. You can then devise a plan to work on each of these skills when your child is calm. You may want to create a reward system to support them with learning each new skill if they are not overly motivated to do so. Incorporating their interests into a reward system is often important, to hook your child into it
'Tag team'	Our children's anger can be difficult to manage – particularly when outbursts last for a long time. This can result in even the strongest parent shifting out of a compassionate state and starting to struggle to parent in the way they'd like to. Therefore, if at all possible, it can be helpful to 'tag team' in a compassionate manner with your partner, a trusted family member or a friend during your child's angry episode. Each of you can take a turn with your child and then you can swap over when you feel you need a bit of time out, to re-regulate your emotions once more

The last step of EASE is to look at your '**E' emotions now**, to see how you have got on with creating a plan to manage your child's anger. You can ask yourself:

- Is there a change in the emotions that were initially triggered?

- Do I need to take any more 'A' actions to soothe strategies to help myself with these emotions?

- Have I been able use a compassionate framework to consider my own feelings and my child's struggles?

- Is there anything else I need to support me in this process?

In summary, compassionate parenting can work really well with a variety of childhood struggles, including (but not limited to):

- When your child finds it difficult to share

- For toileting accidents

- If your child is a selective eater

- When your child finds it difficult to separate from you

- For your child's angry outbursts

Bibliography

Bartoshuk, L.M., Duffy, V.B., Miller, I.J. (1994). PTC/PROP Tasting: Anatomy, Psychophysics and Sex Effects. *Physiology Behaviour*, 56, 1165–1171.

Beaufort, E., Welford, M. (2020). *The Kindness Workbook: Creative and compassionate ways to boost your wellbeing*. Robinson.

Best, T., Herring, L., Clarke, C., Kirby, J., Gilbert, P. (2021). The experience of loneliness: the role of fears of compassion and social safeness. *Personality and Individual Differences*, 183.

Bevilacqua, L., Kelly, Y., Heilmann, A., Priest, N., Lacey, R.E. (2021). Adverse childhood experiences and trajectories of internalizing, externalizing and prosocial behaviours from childhood to adolescence. *Child Abuse & Neglect*, 112.

Bowlby, J. (1969). *Attachment. Attachment and loss: Vol 1. Loss.* New York: Basic Books.

Bryson, T., Siegel, D. (2012). *The Whole-Brain Child*. Robinson.

Dawes, L., Gorringe, N., Russell, L., Hodson, K., Swanston, J., Wimshurst, S. (2018). *Brighter Futures: A Parent's Guide to Raising Happy, Confident Children in the Primary School Years*. Free Association Books.

Duchovic, C.A., Gerkensmeyer, J.E., Jingwei, B.C. (2009). Factors associated with parental distress. *Journal of Child and Adolescent Psychiatric Nursing*, 22(1), 40–48.

ERIC (The Children's Bowel and Bladder Charity): https://eric.org.uk

Feingold, B. (1985). *Why Your Child is Hyperactive: The bestselling book on how ADHD is caused by artificial food flavors and colors*. Random House USA Inc.

Gerhart, S. (2004). *Why Love Matters*. Routledge.

Gilbert, P. (2009). *The Compassionate Mind*. Constable.

Gilbert, P. (2014). The origins and nature of compassion focused therapy. *British Journal of Clinical Psychology*, 53, 6–41.

Gilbert, P. (2020). Compassion: From its evolution to a psychotherapy. *Frontiers of Psychology* (11). Available from: http://dol.org/10.3389/fpsyg.2020.586161

Harris, G. (2018). Food Neophobia: Behavioural and Biological Influences: Neophobia at 20 months: a visual categorisation problem? *Behavioural and Biological Influences*, 193–217.

Harris, R. (2008). *The Happiness Trap: How to stop struggling and start living*. Trumpeter Books.

Heins, T., Richie, K. (1983). Beating Sneaky Poo: ideas for faecal soiling. https://dulwichcentre.com.au/beating-sneaky-poo-1.pdf

Hoang, N-P.T., Kirby, J.N., Haslam, D.M., Sanders, M.R. (2022). Promoting Positive Relationship between parents and grandparents: a randomised controlled trial of group Triple P plus Compassion in Vietnam. *Behavior Therapy*, 53 (6), 1175–1190.

Irons, C., Beaumont, E. (2017). *The Compassionate Mind Workbook: A step by step guide to developing your compassionate self*. Robinson.

Kirby, J. (2019). Nurturing Family Environments for Children: Compassion-focused parenting as a form of parenting intervention. *Education Sciences*, 10, 3.

Kirby, J.D., Kirkland, K., Wilks, M., Green, M. (2023). Testing the bounds of compassion in young children. *Royal Society Open Science*, 10 (2).

Kuypers, L. (2011). *The Zones of Regulation*. Think Social Publishing.

Laube, C., Lorenz, R., van den Bos, W. (2020). Pubertal testosterone correlates with adolescent impatience and dorsal striatal activity. *Developmental Cognitive Neuroscience* 42. Available online on: https://doi.org/10.1016/j.dcn.2019.100749

MacBeth, A., Gumley, A. (2012). Exploring compassion: a meta-analysis of the association between self-compassion and psychopathology. *Clinical Psychology Review*, 32(6), 545–552.

Madeleine McCann https://www.bbc.co.uk/news/uk-england-52910472 disappearance: A timeline, *BBC News*.

Matos, M., Duarte, J., Pinto-Gouveia, J. (2017). The origins of fears of compassion: shame and lack of safeness memories, fears of compassion and psychopathology. *The Journal of Psychology*, 151 (8), 804–819.

Merritt, O.A., Purdon, C.L. (2020). Scared of compassion: fear of compassion in anxiety, mood and non-clinical groups. *British Journal of Clinical Psychology*, 59 (3), 354–368.

Nelsen, J. (2006). *Positive Discipline*. Ballantine Books, New York.

Preston, S. D. (2013). The origins of altruism in offspring care. *Psychological Bulletin*, 139, 1305–1341. Available from: DOI: 10.1037/a0031755

Roberts, G., Bahnson, H., du Toit, G., Brittain, E., Plaut, M., Lack, G. (2023). Defining the window of opportunity to prevent peanut allergy. *Journal Allergy Clinical Immunology*. May: 151(5), 1329–1336.

Strauss, C., Taylor, B.L., Gu, J., Kuyken, W., Baer, R., Jones, F. et al. (2016). What is compassion and how can we measure it? A review of definitions and measures. *Clinical Psychology Review*, 47, 15–27. Available from: DOI: 10.1016/j.cpr.2016.05.004

Welford, M., Langmead, K. (2015). Compassion-based initiatives in educational settings. *Education and Child Psychology*, 32 (1), 71–80.

https://www.uks port.gov.uk/news/2015/05/12/we-need-you-british-athletes-on-the-importance-of-home-crowd-support

https://www.bpinetwork.org/thought-leadership/studies/67

https://www.bbc.co.uk/news/uk-england-52910472

Index